CONTENTS

INTRODUCTION	6
1 DEFINE YOUR OBJECTIVES	19
2 BUDGET, RUNNING COSTS, CAN YOU SUPPORT YOURSELF?	34
3 SIZE MATTERS	48
4 WHAT SHOULD MY BOAT BE MADE OF?	62
5 HULL DESIGN	91
6 THE RIG	122
7 THE ENGINE AND MECHANICALS	145
8 WHAT FEATURES ARE ESSENTIAL, DESIRABLE, UNNECESSARY	166
9 HOW SHOULD I GO ABOUT FINDING MY BOAT	189
10 QUALIFICATIONS AND INSURANCE	202
11 NAVIGATION EQUIPMENT	213
12 SAFETY EQUIPMENT, TENDERS, BACKUPS AND SPARE EVERYTHING	222
13 SURVEYS AND SAFETY CHECKS	246

14 WHERE WILL I KEEP IT - MARINAS AND
                               ANCHORAGES   250

15 THE LIVEABOARD LIFESTYLE – CONCLUSIONS   259

16 CHECKLIST TO TAKE TO VIEWINGS   280

LIST OF PHOTOGRAPHS

The author aboard Yacht Francesca	6
Bringing Yacht Francesca to England	8
The canal basin Gravesend	12
The marina at Herrang	14
Approaching Cape St Vincent	15
Shipwreck	17
A broad beam barge	19
A Humber Keel sailing barge	20
Narrow boats	21
A liveaboard tug boat	23
A modern liveaboard barge	23
Shrimping Trawler converted to liveaboard	25
A Passage Maker	26
A long range motor boat	27
A converted fishing vessel	28
Interior of a static liveaboard	28
Anodes	35
Yacht Francesca in Ventotene	38
Lifting keel trailer sailer	51
Fin keel yacht on a trailer	52
A selection of trailer sailers	53
Yacht Francesca in Cartagena plus Superyacht	55

Trimaran	58
Catamaran with two wind generators and in mast furling	60
Classic wooden liveaboard yacht	62
Steel liveaboard yacht	63
Aluminium liveaboard yacht	64
Living aboard out of the water	68
Fin keel with damage	70
Large steel liveaboard sailing boat in Elba	75
Aluminium liveaboard cutter rig with wheelhouse, wind generator and radar	78
Nicholson 38 foot fibreglass ketch	81
Modern fibreglass production yacht	83
Nauticat 38 wheelhouse ketch	85
Ferro cement gaff rig cutter	87
The problems with ferro cement	89
Yacht Francesca making good progress under sail	92
Typical fin keel	93
Bilge keels	93
Drop keel and bow thruster	94
Modern high performance fibreglass yacht	95
Lovely cutter ketch with canoe stern	101
Propeller and rudder protected by long keel	102
Long keel out of the water	103
Daggerboard catamaran	104
Rescuing a fin keel yacht run aground	108
Yacht Francesca out of the water	110
Mediterranean marina mooring system	111
Scandinavian marina moorings	112
Sailing barge in the Dutch canals	116
Dismasted catamaran	119
Spinnaker difficulties	122
Modern sloop in light winds	124

Ripped sail difficulties	127
Going up the mast	129
Catamaran with sail bag attached to the boom	130
Yacht Francesca running under Genoa	132
Candy striping on a furled Genoa	133
Yacht Francesca under full sail	136
Yawl rigged yacht	138
Rare schooner rigged liveaboard yacht	141
Classic gaff rigged yacht	142
Engine Bay	147
Ship constrained by draft	148
Broken gearbox component	155
Keel cooling pipe	163
Water maker	167
Holding tank	177
Hot water tank with calorifier (immersion heater)	180
Diesel stove	183
Folding bicycle	188
The author way back when on a training course	203
Old GPS, modern sonar	213
Courtesy flag, spreaders and radar	220
Safety equipment on deck	224
Safety harness	226
My home made passerelle and EPIRB	230
Plastic tender with outboard motor	238
My Tinker ready to sail	240
RIB and Walker Bay	243
Anchorage in Greece	257
Corinth Canal	263
Minke Whale	264
Fishing boat at sunrise	265
Delos	266

Pilot Whales	267
Eagle Owl resting aboard	268
Dutch windmill at night	269
Octopus drying in the Greek islands	270
Volcano at sunset	271
Making your mark in The Azores	272
Risso's Dolphin	273
Kayaking on the Guadiana River	274
Deserted anchorage	275
Gulf Of Corinth	276
Cleaning your hull	277

INTRODUCTION

Thank you for buying my book, I hope you find it useful. All the opinions expressed here are basically my own, primarily they are based on my personal experiences, although in some cases coloured by discussions I've had with other yachtsmen and women, I met on my travels, who told me about their own, often different experiences. A common conversation in marina bars and anchorages the world over!

The author hard at work in the wheelhouse of his boat in Bulgaria 2010.

The book is intended to be a discussion about the, style of boat, its features and equipment. Feel free to disagree with my conclusions, if nothing else the points raised are worthy of consideration before you go spending thousands of hard earned pounds, dollars, euros etc. Not to mention risking your life and possessions on the high seas, assuming international travel is one of your objectives. It most certainly was one of mine. You may also find yourself transporting friends or loved ones on occasion; they may be prepared to take the same risks as you, but you will feel a responsibility, it's only human, so having a boat that is fit for purpose matters.

The previous owner of my boat accompanied me from Waterford in Southern Ireland to Gravesend on the River Thames in December! Here we are motoring in a calm English Channel after a pretty stormy crossing of the Irish Sea.

I bought my boat in 2003 and moved aboard immediately, I sold her in 2013 and made a final delivery voyage with the new owner, enabling him to see how everything works; when I bought her, Peter the owner before me did the same for me. When you buy your boat it may be in the place you wish to spend the first months getting to know your way around, but if the boat is elsewhere, then an initial voyage with the previous owner on board is very helpful indeed. If the previous owner is reluctant to help in that way I'd suggest making sure they have a very good reason, such as illness, or infirmity, or maybe they inherited the boat, know little about it and just need to sell it, however if they're fit and able and have been using the boat, but don't want to do a voyage with you I'd smell a rat and be tempted to walk away, however much of a bargain it appears to be.

On the subject of trust a little bit about my experience. I'm not a boat designer or naval architect, but I am a guy who has gone through what you're planning to do. I purchased my boat in Waterford in Southern Ireland late in the year.

After looking at at least a dozen boats and paying for three surveys. It wasn't as simple as I thought it would be! I wanted to get my new boat to a marina in the canal basin at Gravesend in Kent before Christmas so that I could move everything I planned on taking from my house in Kent, get it aboard, put the rest into storage, move onto the boat myself and rent the house out. A big part of my strategy for making this lifestyle work for me was to have an income from my house, (I'll be talking about that and alternative ways to make ends meet in Chapter 15).

Anyhow Peter and I took the boat from Waterford to Gravesend in December. Yes, we crossed the notorious Irish Sea in December and it lived up to its reputation, but if a vendor is prepared to do that, so long as you've established their credentials as a sailor, then it inspires confidence. Peter had previously taken the boat from Europe as far as Venezuela on his adventures with her, so he was no novice and he had faith in the seaworthiness of his, soon to be my,boat.

We left Waterford with a good forecast and set a course directly for Lands End intending to go non stop. Of course the forecast was wrong and the Irish Sea did what the Irish Sea does and in quite horrible conditions we changed course for the safe harbour of Milford Haven in Wales. This book won't be dealing with passage planning or anything of that sort but it will suggest a minimum level of qualifications and competence.

We got safely into Milford Haven and stayed there for several days before the storm abated and we made the rest of the journey in delightful conditions. Having since survived a Tropical Storm, which to my mind (and going by my instruments) was hurricane force when it hit me in mid Atlantic I'm sure my boat would have made it to Lands End and beyond, but when there's a safe harbour in the offing best to take it.

I started making some changes and making some improvements suggested by the surveyor, whilst I was at Gravesend, then took the boat to South Dock Marina in London as I was expecting guests from the USA and I figured they'd rather be in London. I made several new sailing friends at South Dock, Coppercoated the hull, installed back up steering, bought the extra equipment I wanted, had an RYA Safety Check, took some extra training (see Chapters 10 and 13) and finally everything was in place for me to set off. For the first few legs of the voyage various friends accompanied me usually only one at a time but for the leg from Scotland to Sweden two friends joined me.

My boat in the canal basin at Gravesend where I started to make her my own. At this point she still carries her previous name and previous port of registration Bremmerhaven. Notice also that the Zodiac inflatable is hung sideways to decrease the length of the yacht, you can see the slatted floor. Tenders and dinghies are discussed in detail much later in the book.

Later on I would do thousands of miles solo and my boat was set up for solo sailing with all running rigging terminating in the wheelhouse. Although things would sometimes snag or go wrong, necessitating trips to the bow in big waves, nonetheless I love wheelhouses, the protection they give is marvellous, especially if you travel in rough seas, to colder climes or in winter generally. However, that's a discussion point for Chapter 5 really.

From London I voyaged out of the Thames and up the East Coast of England to the border with Scotland. My friend David O'Brien joined me for that leg. Off Lowestoft we experienced the second worst storm and possibly the most dangerous of my ten years, but we survived it. The waves in the North Sea can be very steep on account of the shallowness of that region, quite a different shape from Atlantic waves. Dave went home from Barrow and Ken Townsend joined me to sail to Northern Scotland, we had beautiful conditions. When Ken went home two other friends from dancing joined me and we crossed the North Sea to Norway and then down through The Sound, around Southern Norway and Sweden and up to the Swing Dance Festival at Herrang in the Baltic, north of Stockholm.

There's an interesting anecdote about marina fees related to that. The Swing Dance Festival at Herrang lasts a month. This would be my third and to date last visit. One of the organisers then was a delightful chap called Leonard. I phoned him in the March and told him I'd be coming. He asked me why I was phoning him so far in advance. I said I would be coming by yacht from England and that I wanted to be sure to get a berth in the marina for the entire month.

The marina at Herrang, the location of the world's foremost swing dance festival! One of the innumerable possibilities owning your own boat offers, although for this one you can fly to Stockholm and rent a car or take a bus, but it's not the same!

He called me back a few days later and told me he'd booked me in for a year! I asked him why on earth had he done that? He said that for a month I'd pay a day rate and it added up to more than the cost for a year, so he'd taken a year on my behalf. A bit of homework always pays off, which I guess is why you bought this book.

Approaching Cape St Vincent.

From the Northern Baltic I sailed to Southern Portugal, all in the first year of serious travelling! After that I sailed the Mediterranean all the way to the Middle East and back via North Africa. Before reaching the Middle East I went through the Dardanelles and the Bosphorus and cruised the Black Sea. I took a break from sailing my own boat and did a yacht delivery from Gibraltar to Antigua and finally I sailed my own yacht out the The Azores, up to the Isles Of Scilly and finally to Gallion's Reach Marina in London.

After visiting some supposedly dangerous places on my travels the boat was comprehensively burgled in London. The marina website said they had CCTV and a 24hour guard. In fact when I was there they had neither. I lost most of my mementoes from my travels, presents for friends and much more besides, they even prised the clock and barometer off the bulkhead.

The local police were worse than useless, they asked me to list everything that had been stolen so they could look out for it. That exercise took me about forty eight hours of clearing up and looking for things. When I took my list to the nominated Police Station I was told they didn't want it any more, they'd closed the case as unsolvable due to the absence of CCTV! A retired police officer, friend of a friend, later told me they cannot simply close a case like that and that I should write to the Chief Constable, but that was too many years later to do me any good.

In a depressed state I sold my boat cheaply, before the appalling marina asked for a renewal fee! At least I enjoyed the delivery, back to Lowestoft as it happened, but no storms this time. The next summer a sailing friend I'd met in Turkey asked me to help deliver his boat from Santa Maria De Leuca in southern Italy to Marseilles as he was selling up too. That was a lovely, gentle six week trip and I haven't sailed since.

It's now 2019 and I've been thinking about writing this book for a while. A friend has asked me to do it and she's not the first, plus the sea is in my blood and I'm thinking about buying another boat myself so this will focus the mind, and if it helps others too, then all well and good.

I'd encourage you to go for it. You're obviously thinking about it, otherwise there'd be no point in reading this. Once you've looked at all the chapters and complexities you might feel a bit daunted. Don't be. You don't have to take my advice, you have to take responsibility for your own choices, just as you do in an Atlantic storm. It's easy to buy something if you've saved the money, living with it, if it's a boat anyway, and making it work for you requires a lot of thought and research. However, you've made a start! Where there's a will there IS a way and if you want something badly enough you will achieve it.

Every year big ships are lost, treat the oceans and seas with the respect they deserve and then a little more for good measure, this is in the Black Sea.

The sea is a dangerous place, the world's oceans have been vast graveyards since time immemorial. Treat it with all the respect it deserves and then some. I've found that when I'm living life in the fast lane, that's when I feel most alive. I've been a skydiving instructor, raced single seater cars and motorcycles and sailed thousands of blue water miles. I'm very glad I'm not dead, but will I keep taking risks? You betcha.

At a marina party in Spain I danced the Lindy Hop enthusiastically with a partner who knew the dance as well as I did. Immediately afterwards a Norwegian lady in her mid nineties came up and asked me to dance with her. After dancing with her we fell into conversation. She had sailed through the Straits of Magellan at the age of 90! There's always someone who's gone further, achieved more, taken on bigger challenges, but life's not a competition. That lady was an inspiration to me and still is. Take it a day at a time, get opinions and advice from others and you'll achieve your goals. Now go get that boat!

CHAPTER 1
DEFINE YOUR OBJECTIVES

The first friend who asked me about buying a boat to liveaboard actually wanted a broad beam barge to live on. She wanted a working engine so she could move it, but no masts or rigging so far fewer complications. Of course a broad beam barge (broad beam just means wide) can make a wonderful home. All that cargo space can translate into a very spacious (for a boat) amount of living area. What a broad beam barge cannot do is travel the canals in the UK, you need a narrow boat for that, but a broad beam barge can navigate rivers and French canals for example, plus many in the Netherlands and other places. So knowing what you want to do and where you want to go is important.

A broad beam barge in The Netherlands, a good place to look if that's what you want, and a good place to start from if the waterways of Europe are your goal.

This book is primarily for people who want to travel internationally on the high seas, but considerations about draft, that is the depth of the boat or the depth of water it needs under it so as to not touch the bottom may still apply, especially in canals. The height will matter too if you're going to want to pass under low bridges. The condition it is in will certainly apply, as will what it's made of, budget and the equipment you ideally want on board to make living on board a practical proposition.

I met the then owners of Gainsborough Trader in London, she's what's known as a Humber keeled barge, which means she has a flat bottom basically and sails thanks to the lee boards which drop down. She's a very famous Dunkirk Small Ships boat, saved from the scrap yard and converted into a stunning luxurious and quite large home. Clearly she can cross The Channel in the right conditions but she'd be hard work solo and she wouldn't handle rough seas terribly well. Wonderful home though.

Narrow boats are a very British phenomenon more restricted for space than a broad beam barge they can nonetheless make a characterful and practical home. They can travel far and wide in the UK, far more so than a broad beam barge, and if transported across The Channel can tackle the canals of Europe too.

Most surviving old barges and narrow boats which once carried cargo have been converted into liveaboards, but new purpose built boats, of both types, have been in production for many years too. At the time of writing it's possible to buy a brand new fifty foot narrow boat, completely fitted out with beds, storage, cooker, heating, fridge freezer and other mod cons for a hundred thousand pounds. At the other end of the spectrum an old fibreglass Norfolk Broads holiday cruiser, probably an ex hire boat and in need of some renovation might be had for less than a thousand pounds and there must be thousands of alternatives in between.

If you're an engineer or particularly good with your hands a doer upper may be an option, if not keep saving until you have enough for something half way decent to start with. I say half way decent because it's a fact that boats, like classic cars and motorcycles nearly always want some job or other doing, but it's the big jobs that will cost you.

An old tug boat can make a spacious and characterful home, and of course it can be moved from place to place, but it's not the ideal tool to cross oceans.

A broad beam barge like this can make a cavernous and beautiful home, it can also travel many rivers and canals in Europe so it is a travelling liveaboard, even internationally, but not trans ocean.

It may seem a bit over the top but write down what you think you want, be it barge, narrow boat, classic yacht, sailing barge, a passage maker, a nice boat to live on permanently in a marina, a houseboat even. Many years ago I considered buying a converted tug boat, primarily because it came with a mooring at Hammersmith in London and represented an affordable and characterful way to live in the expensive capital city. That was before I decided to go sailing. Someone else got there first in that instance.

From the list above you may be wondering what a passage maker is. A passage maker is effectively a motor boat with the seaworthiness and fuel capacity, ie range to cross oceans. If you can afford the fuel and you don't want to mess around with sails, but you do want to go long distances that could be something you'd want to look into. You can buy purpose built passage makers or converted fishing boats. I've met a few people with them. On the East Mediterranean Yacht Rally I met some Americans on a very luxurious and large, purpose built passage maker. In the Mediterranean I met an English guy on a very tastefully converted old wooden shrimping trawler.

In the Balearics I made friends with a guy living on this converted Shrimping Trawler. It might not have met every requirement for a true Passage Maker but it had already done thousands of miles and had been made into a beautiful character home. Being made of wood the maintenance costs would have been too much for me, but if you are, for example, retired and don't want to bother with sails and have the money required for fuel and maintenance, something like this might suit you.

This is a true Passage Maker with stabilisers, the lot.

Use Google to find out more about passage makers if you think that's your bag. There's at least one book on the subject, probably more by now. If memory serves, the term was coined by an ex American sea captain, who, after retiring wanted to travel by sea but didn't want what he saw as the hassle of sails. He basically came up with a formula for a boat to qualify as what he called a passage maker. From memory he came up with something called the trawler truth ratio, he defined what the range should be and certain safety considerations, for example it should have two engines with independent gear boxes and prop shafts in case of failure. This isn't a book about passage makers specifically, I looked into it once and the above is what I remember, more or less. However, it won't take you long to find out all about them as a class of boat, if you see things as he did.

For me the fuel to run a passage maker would be too expensive, the wind is free and I know how sails work already so for most of this book I'll be discussing sailing boats in one form or another. I also like the peace and tranquillity that accompanies travel under sail, in good conditions anyway! If a passage maker, narrow boat, tug or other class of boat appeals to you certain sections of what follows will still, I hope, prove useful to you.

This may not have every feature of an official Passage Maker but it had come from Canada. She was pretty new, very spacious and luxurious. Not for the budget conscious though.

This sort of thing has the potential to be a Passage Maker, but was in fact a stationary home.

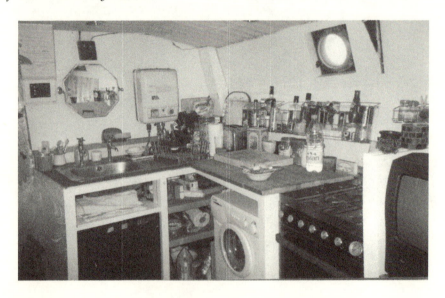

An interior like this means all the convenience of living on land, but it's not practical in a rough sea, this boat isn't for the travelling liveaboard.

Now, sailors and soon to be sailors in particular. Make a list of your objectives. It might seem a bit over the top to write them down, but it focusses the mind and it's a useful document to refer back to when you start the serious business of looking at boats. And you should look at as many as you need to. However, you don't want to waste your time, or that of others, so narrowing the parameters to what might prove acceptable to you is a very good idea. You probably don't want to be looking at eighteen footers, or even probably twenty seven footers if you plan to go very long distances with a partner or companion.

It can be done; the book Shrimpy, by Shane Acton gives you a very good example of how it CAN be done. In fact when I was much younger it very much inspired me, but I was too busy being a skydiving instructor in the 1970s. It's out of print and my copy is not for sale, but if you can find an example online it's a very good read indeed. However if you're not a young, adventurous, fit, ex Royal Marine you'll probably want something a little more robust and comfortable than his eighteen foot plywood Caprice, despite what he achieved with it.

So write it down, where do you want to go? Does it involve crossing oceans? Will you ever be solo? Do you need space for guests? Do you want to go up rivers like the Seine, the Duro, the Guadiana or Guadilquivir? Will you want to navigate the Dutch canals, for example, there's a very nice mast up route from the Isselmeer to Ijmuden via Amsterdam and although the bridges open to accommodate your mast or masts it can be a bit shallow in places so a deep boat can't do it. A small boat like a McGregor 27 with a lifting keel can come equipped with a winch to lower the mast single handedly, it can go almost anywhere, although it's just a few inches too wide for UK canals. That said I would personally cross the English Channel in one, but not the Atlantic.

Writing down your objectives and then studying the pros and cons described in the following chapters will help you refine your search in terms of the type of boat, size of boat, material it's made from, keel design, rig and sail plan and onboard equipment. You may feel at the end of the exercise that you want a heck of a lot and there's no way you can afford it, but at the time of writing the market is somewhat depressed and bargains are out there. In addition if you decide you want a forty footer or a spacious catamaran, but it's way out of your budget remember that boats depreciate with age and frankly condition is more important than the year of manufacture.

Look at a few boats and you'll see some with rust and dirt everywhere and others with bilges you could eat from and gleaming engine bays. Personally I'd sooner an old boat that's been properly serviced and loved than a nearly new boat that's been abused, or left standing, things work better as a rule when they are used frequently.

Some Canadian friends I met while travelling had bought a brand new boat from a famous and highly respected UK manufacturer. As experienced sailors they had told the manufacturer their precise requirements and had visited the factory several times during the build. Given their very substantial budget, the fact that everything was brand new and their responsible approach, what could possibly go wrong? Well plenty actually, just as an example the manual told the owners to check the bilge pumps after a certain length of time, however at least one of the bilge pumps was so poorly located that my friend had to cut a hatch in one of the bulkheads to get anywhere near it! Brand new boat!

Don't be scared of second, third or fourth hand boats, previous owners will have ironed out the bugs and smart owners have usually made improvements. Look at the person selling the boat almost as much as the boat itself and don't be scared to grill them about their experience, what they've done with the boat and any modifications they've made. I've come across a couple of people who've changed the original rig to a Chinese junk rig. Junk is an unfortunate word, but for solo sailing a junk rig is a very practical option.

What it boils down to is make a list of what your objectives are, consider the specification you're ideally looking for. Let's just say, for the sake of argument, after reading the pros and cons of different designs and materials in this book, and how hard or how easy they are to manage, that you've decided you ideally want a fibreglass boat, cutter ketch rigged, between thirty five and forty feet with a wheelhouse, internal and external steering positions, long keel, a strong engine, large fuel and drinking water tanks, maybe two of each in case one becomes contaminated, holding tanks for black and grey water, solar panels and a wind generator, maybe a diesel generator too. Starting batteries, domestic batteries, a good recent survey, a guest cabin, heating by stove or Webasto/Eberspacher type heating, hot water for washing from shore power and from engine or generator when at sea. AIS, radar, radio and a full set of modern navigation aids, depth sounder, gps chart plotter with charts of almost the whole world!

You now know a specification which meets your EVERY need and want. Such a boat will be out there somewhere and many others will come close. It doesn't have to be the above specification, for your own personal needs you might want something smaller, or even larger, you might choose a steel boat or a catamaran, but work out what you think will work best for you, maybe a couple or more options you'd be prepared to accept and start doing viewings. Include boats which come close, you can usually add a holding tank, wind generator, solar panels if you want to later and if it's missing things you need, then use that when negotiating the price. Actually electronics are one of the few things that have come down in price over the years so you may be able to afford to put in precisely what you want in regard to navigation, depth sounders, radio etc.

Don't buy the first boat you see, however tempting, make it clear that you will be buying a boat, unquestionably. This marks you out as a serious buyer and for many vendors who are tired of dreamers wasting their time they'll be happy to answer all the questions on the list appended at the end of this book. Knowing that you're serious and that you're looking at other boats and that you're asking pertinent, sensible, serious questions they'll probably be flexible on the price. You become the serious buyer they've been waiting for, sometimes for months, and they know they're competing for your cash. At the time of writing there are more boats available than there are serious buyers, so you might actually get everything you want at a price you can afford after all! Good luck!

CHAPTER 2
BUDGET, RUNNING COSTS, CAN YOU SUPPORT YOURSELF?

All boats have costs attached to ownership, so whatever your budget leave a sizeable sum aside for unexpected bills. In addition make sure you have a budget for mooring and insurance as a minimum. I spent £38,000 on my first yacht, but by the time I'd painted her, Coppercoated the hull, fitted new anodes, added emergency back up tiller steering and an outboard bracket, serviced the heater, painted and varnished up top, renewed sails, liferaft and life jackets, purchased electronic and paper charts, new flares, danbuoy, devised a man overboard recovery system and countless other small things she owed me £50,000 and I still had £23,000 set aside for future costs plus an income from rental property which I hoped would clear £1000 per month.

Nice new anodes and plenty of them, on my newly Coppercoated hull, plus many other preparations meant yacht Francesca was ready for a very extended period in the water and travelling.

In fact being a landlord isn't simple, especially if you're at sea and need someone else ie an estate agent to run things for you so the £23,000 also had to cover emergency boiler repairs, new roof tiles or whatever might crop up at my property back in the UK.

Nonetheless I thought I'd been pretty sensible. In fact the £23,000 went down quite dramatically in the first year and I made myself a
 promise that if I ever got down to £5,000 in the bank I'd head home and think again. In fact things stabilised and that didn't happen although it was a close run thing a decade on!

It sounds daunting and it isn't easy I admit. I put all my possessions that were unsuitable for life at sea in storage in my garage. Many of them survived, but one lot of tenants put a ladder on the garage roof, made two holes in it and failed to report it, so many of my things were rain water damaged or totally destroyed. Ironically they'd have been drier on the boat if I'd had the space!

Another tenant broke in and helped himself to a few choice bits, which had survived, before returning abroad. I suppose I was lucky he didn't have a truck! If you're going to have to pay for storage I suggest you sell all but the most sentimental possessions you have and if not saleable chuck them out. The cost of a few years storage will in most cases be more than the cost of replacement and of course the TV, stereo and much of what I'd stored became obsolete while I was away anyhow.

Despite owning it even my storage wasn't really free, since I could have rented the garage out with the house and charged more, so clearing your life out may be tough if you're a hoarder like me, but it makes good financial sense. I did sell quite a lot to make my dreams come true, a classic car and a classic motorcycle and my father's collection of very, very early telephones. That last I regretted but they'd only have been water damaged or nicked, so logically I did the right thing. If you have to make sacrifices to achieve your liveaboard, boat gypsy lifestyle you'll appreciate it even more than someone born rich. Everything you sell gets you closer to making it happen and giving you the flexibility you will need.

At the time of writing I could buy a boat like mine ie same age as mine was back then, same size and similar or better condition for about £20,000, that's how much the market has changed, so don't be disheartened. Since the condition may well be that bit better and given that you're going to use the checklist supplied at the end of this book and learn from my experiences to avoid mistakes, let's hope you won't have to spend as much as I did before you head off. Even so keeping £10-15,000 of your budget aside to make things how you want them to be after purchasing your boat still makes sense. Then you need your buffer against the unforeseen, boats have come down in price, but many other things have gone up in price, so let's say £30,000, and you need an income, at least £1000 per month, more if you can.

In other words given an income while travelling I think I could comfortably start over and repeat the exercise if I had £65,000 available. I'm not saying that should be your budget, you may want a larger, or smaller boat, you might be planning as a couple, you may have the wherewithal to buy new, or like one brave German I met travelling solo in a 23 foot boat you might be that bit braver and more adventurous than I am and need less money.

Yacht Francesca anchored at Ventotene in the beautiful Aeolian islands, reasonably safe and totally free.

I tended to use marinas in winter when they're cheaper and travel and anchor in bays and rivers throughout the summer, unless I needed to go in for fuel or drinking water, or if there wasn't a suitable anchorage I would use whatever harbour or marina was available. Using marinas as little as possible in peak season is a good strategy. In fact I also kept travelling for most of one winter too. I did find a couple of unfinished marinas in Greece that were safe and free, but don't bank on it! Life at anchor can be complicated too; unsurprisingly I'd recommend my previous book 'How To Anchor Safely – So You Sleep Well!'.

Being a landlord is one way you might expect to get some capital growth and an income (a good target to aim for) and you might be luckier than I was. Given what happened to me however, I wouldn't do it that way again.

My Canadian friends with the large new yacht which had some teething troubles, as mentioned earlier, had sold up their home. At the time I thought my way was better, especially given the depreciation on a new boat, but they had a more comfortable, larger and faster boat than mine and despite those teething troubles everything down to the last nut and bolt was brand new, so less maintenance at least in the short term. I never asked them their financial situation, well, you don't do you. However I'm pretty certain they'd kept themselves a sensible buffer for future life changes.

On my travels I met some noticeably very rich people and others clearly with less to work with than me. On the whole there's not a lot of snobbery amongst liveaboard boat gypsies, which is how I saw myself and there is a lot of helping each other out, sharing tools and in some marinas a 'radio net' at a set time each morning where people can buy, sell, ask for help or offer help.

I'm not a financial advisor so I won't presume to advise on any specific investments. I have now sold my house and invested roughly half the money in dividend paying company shares. The value may go up or down of course but in point of fact after the ravages of several tenants and despite my swiftly sending money for whatever needed doing whenever the estate agent asked for it my house did not achieve anything near the valuation. Being in Kent, the current Brexit blight will have had something to do with that, but even property is a risk these days.

The other half is in interest earning bank accounts, of course rates are very low and my combined income from dividends and interest is probably going to work out less than the theoretical rental income, BUT, and it's a big but, the money that comes in is mine I don't have to send it back to pay for roof repairs, new fences, or a new fridge freezer or cooker, or gas safety check, or electrical safety check, or Legionnaires disease safety check for goodness sake!

Governments have assumed landlords are all rich nasty bastards, even those who've worked for years to pay off a mortgage and then downsized from a six figure house to a five figure boat. As a result of this assumption, politicians, in the UK anyway, have gradually made things tougher and tougher for all landlords. Now of course UK politicians bemoan the lack of affordable rented accommodation. That's the intelligence of politicians.

Then there are the tenants that stop paying, and even if they've broken the contract, should the heating fail you still have to stump up and fix it for them, by law, despite the fact that they're living in your house for free! Should you need to evict them, they may well get legal aid, you assuredly won't.

In my previous life I ran an advertising agency and items I bought for the business were set against tax. Buy your tenant a new washing machine or a new fridge freezer and you'll find it's not allowable. The reason I'm telling you all this is that if you're going to be swanning around the Med, or crossing the Atlantic you want, if at all possible, to be able to count on your income not being demanded back! You may have a pension or an annuity, that's good, if you sell up and can invest in a similar fashion to what I have done, that might work for you too, but you may also be able to supplement your income while you travel.

All of us have different skills. Whilst travelling I wrote and self published three books. Two of the other sailors I met on my travels had also published books, they're listed towards the end of this book as suggested further reading; with computers being essential and the internet being available in pretty much all marinas and ports, not to mention cafés and bars it's not as hard as it might seem.

Shane Acton wrote a column for his local newspaper whilst travelling and looked for casual work too in the places he stopped. Even Captain Joshua Slocum gave talks about his travels, as well as writing a book way back in the eighteen hundreds.

These days, rather than write a newspaper column, you're more likely to write a blog about your adventures with pay per click advertising. You can make videos about your travels, about sailing tips, about places and about anything you're prepared to share, such as the loneliness of the long distance sailor, the stresses of being confined together as a couple, home schooling on a boat. People will be interested in these things and you might gain a following. Post these videos to YouTube and promote them on Twitter. So long as you own the copyright and don't film concerts and the like you can allow advertising on your YouTube channel and get paid that way too. Instagram and Pinterest offer further ways to promote your blog and YouTube channel or books.

Personally I also sell my photography on Zazzle, Redbubble and other similar platforms. You'll be in places and seeing things not everyone sees, so if you can take good pictures that can help. The internet provides other work opportunities too, you might be able to build websites, or undertake translation work, proof reading, social media marketing, all these things can be done in a port with WiFi. Maybe you're an artist and you can paint pictures, or you're an artisan and can make things. I met a lady who made jewellery while she travelled and set up shop on crowded beaches every so often. Although she worked a lot with silver, she also worked with shells, so, some at least, of her raw materials were freely available.

A good sailing friend of mine met and married an extraordinarily beautiful lady with a singing voice to match and a talent for the guitar. It wasn't unheard of for her to go ashore busking for a couple of hours and return with €400! Another friend, Terry, living on a ferro cement yacht is a terrific carpenter and finds work on fellow sailors' boats, the finish he achieves and his varnishing skills are phenomenal. If you want an interior to die for, he's your man. I myself have paid a fellow sailor who was a qualified electrician to do an electrical repair to my boat that quite simply baffled me. Before I sailed from London, but whilst living aboard I supplemented my income by doing film extras work, stand in work and small roles. I also gave dancing lessons. Skills, we all have something to offer.

So it goes on, but you need a strategy. You will need to make money, or have an unearned income for food, diesel fuel, (even if you mostly sail as I did, you'll still need to use the motor in harbours and so on and it can get you out of trouble occasionally too, not to mention the fact that you may have diesel fuelled heating on board). You'll need money for marinas, fuel for your outboard, insurance, engine oil and service items, maintenance, breakages, replacement sails and even if you're happy to wear rags, occasionally you'll need to buy something! I hate that expression unearned income I used it for clarity, but to my mind if you've worked hard, saved and invested then the return on investment IS earned. I used the term to differentiate income that comes in more or less automatically, even while you're asleep, from that which you might earn as you go along.

On that subject once more it had occurred to me when planning my adventure that I might charge to take people sailing for a day. I'm writing this in June 2019 and we Brits are still European citizens so the right to work in most European countries isn't and wasn't then an issue. If Brexit goes through that probably won't be the case for Brits. However, to take fare paying customers legally in this litigious age you should probably have a Yachtmaster qualification with commercial endorsement, first aid and so on and then you'll need to look at your insurance. Friends came on board my boat and some made a contribution to my costs, but I never got into the business of charging for trips.

I've met yachties who did though and whilst I'm not recommending anything illegal you will meet people who'd like to go out on your boat, it's up to you how you handle that. I met one couple who offered crewed charters on their boat, I didn't enquire as to their qualifications and insurance but I didn't want to do that personally with my boat anyway, it was first and foremost my home and I didn't want to have someone else on board calling the shots. Your boat, your call though.

Getting back to the right to work, that may be lost to Brits in twenty seven other European countries if Brexit goes ahead, but for European citizens casual work as a waiter, bar person, cleaner, driver, farm hand, labourer, builder, painter and decorator, interpretor, translator, office worker all these things are possible in many, many places, even in Atlantic islands such as the Canaries and the Azores, particularly if you have at least some language skills to go about advertising yourself, finding agencies and talking to the locals. One sailing friend I made gave English lessons in accredited schools, having attained the necessary qualification before going to sea.

However you support yourself you need to make your financial arrangements as simple as possible. Then there's the mail. If you're lucky enough to have parents alive they will probably provide you with a mailing address and sort out any unexpected bills. I had lost my parents but I did have a good and trustworthy friend, who allowed me to use his address and he was someone I trusted enough to make him a signatory on my bank account and give him a cheque book so that if anything that needed dealing with arrived in the post he could deal with it. If you get rid of any property you're not likely to get the unexpected bills that came my way, making things simpler still. If necessary you can get a post office box and either come home once a year, or have a friend check that for you. I'm sure we all make different arrangements, but you'll need to consider these things. Possibly, if you have dependents you should also make a will.

Apart from property I cleared the decks so to speak, I sold my car and one motorbike and laid up two motorbikes and informed the authorities about them, it's tricky as the UK authorities want you to confirm and sign that you're not using them every single year, but after some wrangling and exchange of letters and recorded telephone calls in which I explained I could be in mid ocean on the due date, they agreed to put a note on the computer and it actually worked! No fines on my return; if you cant get that flexibility get rid of the vehicles, or get a friend or relative to become the registered keeper.

The only insurances I had were on my property and my boat. It starts to become manageable; I cancelled all my standing orders and direct debits so I couldn't go overdrawn while I was in mid ocean and anyway after selling everything I didn't need them. Even my mobile phone was switched to pay as you go and then largely switched off once I left London.

So let's now take it that you've established how you're going to make this lifestyle change work for you AND how much you can afford to spend on a boat with enough left over for changes to said boat and to tide you over whilst you get into your new life. Now we can get on to the meat of the matter and look at some specifics pertaining to the boat itself!

CHAPTER 3
SIZE MATTERS

If you've defined your objectives as already suggested then you may have an idea about what size of boat you really want. Your budget will have a bearing too, but maybe not as much as you might think, if you're prepared to shop around and bide your time.

I bought my boat in the Republic Of Ireland and it's not a bad place to look. Don't just look close at hand. The internet brings the world to your home. I've seen some incredible bargains on internet auction sites and a friend bought a nearly new 32ft boat in Greece for a few thousand Euros. It's not the only bargain Greece has had to offer in the last few years either given the economic difficulties that country has experienced and if you're thinking of sailing in the Med. then starting from there is not the end of the world.

Be aware though that a lot of boats in Greece and the islands seem to carry a US registration and identify an American home port. In other words the VAT hasn't been paid and you'll quite likely be asked to pay VAT on the full new cost of the boat, not what you paid for it second hand, so steer clear, or get the vendor to rectify it first AND provide you with the paperwork to prove it.

Getting back to the main point, what I'm saying is choose a size you believe is right for you and look for it. Don't make assumptions that you cannot get it. Opinions about the size of boat you need have changed down the years. For many years Shane Acton held the record for the smallest boat to circumnavigate the globe, something he did in an 18ft plywood Caprice. The record is even smaller now but this isn't a book for would be record breakers.

In the 1970s a 35ft yacht like mine was considered most luxurious, today they're pretty commonplace and 40ft to 60ft yachts abound too. The difference between a 35 footer and a 40 footer may not sound a great deal to the uninitiated, but the longer boat is also generally wider and deeper, making a very big difference indeed to the internal volume, the space for beds, tables, cookers, fridges, showers, toilets, storage, headroom, equipment. Incidentally mariners still call toilets 'the heads' going back to the days of tall ships when the toilet was usually a hole in the region of the bowsprit, or head of the ship, with a clear drop to the sea below, where sailors did the necessary. Ask a vendor to show you the toilet and he'll know you're a novice, or at least suspect it.

So, an 18ft yacht could and has circumnavigated. Boat design has moved on. I've mentioned the MacGregor 27ft already, it's actually a way smaller hull than my 35 footer, for the reasons mentioned above, the interior space is very impressive however. Part of the reason for this is it's designed to use an outboard motor, so there's no engine room taking up interior space. It's also a little slab sided and it's for these reasons I wouldn't personally choose to cross oceans in one. However, the interior is very cleverly designed with things sliding out of the way when not needed and with a double bed under the cockpit it actually appears very spacious. Two people could liveaboard, especially if they did not have serious travel ambitions. MacGregor have some impressive facts and figures about what the boat can achieve in rough seas and some impressive videos of the boat sailing in heavy seas as well. If you're interested take a look, your choice.

With its lifting keel the MacGregor sits nicely on a trailer, because it uses water as ballast which can be pumped out, it's also quite light. If you're fit enough to scramble inside when it's on the trailer you could use it like a caravan and launch it wherever you wish. With a powerful out board motor the waterways of Europe are also open to you.

If you were to choose a boat which utilises an outboard motor, and some catamarans do that too, bear in mind that petrol is far more flammable, not to say explosive compared with diesel and although not commonplace diesel outboards are available. The MacGregor is classed as a trailer-sailer and of course it's not the only one, mostly from about 18 feet up to the size of the MacGregor or thereabouts. Many, like the Mac have a lifting keel, some have bilge keels. It is possible to trailer a small yacht with a fin keel given a suitable trailer, but again it's uncommon and not really ideal.

Boats with a fixed keel can be trailered, but it's not as easy especially the launch and recovery.

Other trailer sailers are available.

If you have room on your drive and want to experiment before committing to the full liveaboard life, then a trailer-sailer won't attract marina fees while it's at your home and can be used much like a caravan, tow it around Europe and launch in various places, or with a powerful motor, the MacGregor can take outboards up to 50HP, you could do European canals and strongly flowing rivers like the Rhine and the Danube.

My German buddy sailing solo in a very small yacht was using the smallest Beneteau First, there's a similar, but not identical Jenneau too, the same company owns both brands. My friend claimed his boat is unsinkable, they said the same about the Titanic, in this case the claim might be more reasonable, if you broke it clean in half both halves would probably, depending on contents, remain afloat due the the materials used in its construction, a kind of fibreglass sandwich. Just because the bits float I wouldn't want to try living and surviving in half a boat, so I regard it as a bit of an irrelevance.

When we get on to the subject of what your boat should be made from I won't differentiate between types of fibreglass construction for this reason. You may like the sound of the above, but even that has drawbacks if water penetrates the sandwich. The middle buoyant layer could well be balsa wood for example and it won't like prolonged exposure to salt water.

As a general rule, the smaller the boat, the easier it will be to sail. Really large sails are a liability to the single handed sailor in a sudden squall, they're immensely powerful and getting them down or reefing them in a sudden emergency can be hard, especially as that will be the time that something will jam if it's going to.

Yacht Francesca dwarfed by a super yacht in Cartagena, the latter not being for the single hander! When we talk about passing under bridges, remember this picture!

My 35ft boat however had four sails, two foresails, a main and a mizzen, nor were the two masts terribly high, so although the Main and the Genoa were quite large enough, things could have been far worse on a sloop with a single very tall mast and two sails half as big again or more!

So, generally speaking small boats are easier to sail, but not automatically so. Small boats take big waves harder than larger yachts and are more likely to take water over the decks. Very few small boats have protective wheelhouses, they tend to have open cockpits and tillers as a rule. However there are 27 footers and upwards with wheelhouses, again, generally speaking and they tend to be classed as motor-sailers, some will sail well, but again, as a general rule sailing performance isn't what they're about. Really small boats don't normally have the capacity to carry radar, a feature I love to have.

Small boats have more small harbours available to them and anchorages too, but the draft or depth of the boat is often more important, so a small boat with a fin keel will probably be deeper in draft and require deeper water than a larger one with a lifting keel, or a catamaran. However, as a general rule of thumb smaller boats get into more places.

If you want the adventure of a small boat with an open cockpit then as mentioned there are new and nearly new examples out there. However, don't be afraid of an older boat. For many years a British firm called Westerly manufactured a great number of boats. Many were small although they built larger boats as time went on and I'd personally consider any Westerly if the size suited my objectives. The thing is that all their hulls, regardless of size, were certificated by Lloyds of London, in short, they were very well put together when they were new, so if you find one you like and it gets a good survey, I personally wouldn't let the age worry me.

Again personally speaking I wouldn't want to liveaboard AND travel, doing true blue water sailing on anything less than 30ft. I felt my 35 footer was ideal. That was the length of the hull overall, not the waterline length which is less. In fact my bowsprit made my boat somewhat over 35ft, not to mention the dinghy on the back, but I always gave that as the length when I visited marinas. A very few checked and argued, well, about two in ten years!

At Almerimar in Spain they have marks on the quay where you tie up to check in so the staff can look out of the window and check! A bowsprit at the front and a dinghy suspended horizontally on davits at the back add quite a lot to the length of your boat. Most marinas won't quibble. Some bowsprits are retractable which is handy, and you can temporarily suspend your tender on its side if necessary to reduce the length by a couple of feet.

It's a scientific fact that the longer the hull the higher its theoretical top speed, known as hull speed, so if speed is an issue to you think longer, but remember the hull shape and design will play a role too. When I was looking for my first liveaboard I was primarily concerned with safety and comfort, not speed. My next liveaboard boat will be no less than 35ft and if I can find a 40 footer I consider manageable when alone I'd take the extra space. Or maybe a catamaran.

When I first looked for a boat I'll admit to a prejudice against catamarans. On my travels I met several catamaran owners and spent a day with a catamaran designer discussing the pros and cons. We'll come back to those in Chapter 5 when we look at the various types of monohull design as well.

Trimarans are very fast but also extremely wide they're primarily for the racers. In some cases the outside hulls fold in close to the sides of the central hull to make them more practical in a marina or harbour and to keep the mooring cost down, but, generally speaking you're looking at a big boat, with little room inside since the spaces between the hulls are unlikely to be used, or the outriggers themselves. A catamaran uses the space in each hull AND in the bridge between the two.

I still have some issues with multihulls; a trimaran flipped off Portugal while I was there, they were trying to get into the port I'd already entered and tragically there was a fatality. However, after much thought and discussion, I would now consider a catamaran as a blue water liveaboard. The interior space is of an entirely different order, they don't rock very much when at anchor and can get right in close to shore. Marinas tended to charge catamaran owners one and a half times the price they charged for a monohull of the same length when I was travelling, but one or two were starting to ask double. All boats are a compromise and we'll discuss those later, but if you want space, view some catamarans as well as monohulls. You'll be surprised how much space there is in each hull, not just the mid section.

Catamarans tend to be more expensive to buy, but again bargains are out there.

A Catamaran like this offers a great deal of space and comfort. This one has in mast furling for the mainsail which is discussed later, I'd also prefer a daggerboard cat without a trampoline, all will become clear as we progress, nonetheless this is a great liveaboard, especially for the Mediterranean.

My conclusion, and it's just my opinion, but based on experience is that for a blue water travelling liveaboard it wants to be 30ft to 40ft, if you want more space but not the extra length, depth and huge sails of a 50 or 60 footer then look at catamarans. You could consider something bigger than 40ft if you're a couple, but my own view is you won't need it and it'll be restrictive in other ways unless it has a lifting keel. Furthermore if one of you is sick or injured the other one will have to manage it alone.

Now, how about the different types of construction and the various materials used to build boats?

CHAPTER 4
WHAT SHOULD MY BOAT BE MADE OF?

This classic wooden boat was being used as a liveaboard and anchored in front of me in Menorca, lovely thing, traditional gaff rigged, you can just see the gaff, above the boom and about two thirds as long as the boom, two foresails that drop, no roller reefing, so a cutter rig, I'm sure she sailed beautifully, but boats like this tend to be old, so be prepared for a lot of maintenance and if you can't do it yourself, a lot of expense.

The first boat ever made by man was probably a hollowed out tree trunk so the most traditional boat building material is wood. The wooden walls, as they were known, of Nelson's fleet gave way, scant years after Trafalgar to iron clads and dreadnoughts as Turner's moving picture of the Fighting Temerere bears witness.

I encountered this beautiful steel liveaboard in Sardinia, the owner told me she was epoxy coated inside and out. The spray paint finish on the exterior would make the owners of some fibreglass boats jealous, but steel boats like this are not commonplace. In mast furling for the large mainsail once again though.

An aluminium yacht under sail.

Steel then is the second boat building material and that too has evolved with corrosion resistant steels having been developed. The study of metals gave us alloys and today there are aluminium boats, so that's a third material.

Fibreglass yachts are the most common today by far, and with good reason, but even fibreglass is a compromise of sorts, so we'll be looking at the pros and cons of all these materials in this chapter. The final material is ferro cement, that's reinforced concrete in reality and it's very strong and yes a concrete boat does float and they're very cheap second hand, but there's a reason for that too. So let's look at the pros and cons of each material in turn, starting with wood.

Simply the pros of wood are, firstly it can be incredibly strong if constructed properly, secondly wooden boats tend to be character boats, you'll probably get a lot of admiring glances from sailors who wouldn't touch one with a barge pole! I read the book 'To The Baltic With Bob' by Griff Rhys Jones, it wasn't the laugh out loud on every page read I'd been promised, but what really got to me was how this particular sailor looked down his nose at people on boats that weren't wooden classics.

Griff, bless him, appeared to sail every summer, make a list of what needed doing and then give his classic yacht to a boat yard for the winter. That's great, if that's all you want to achieve and if you have sufficient wealth for that lifestyle. Griff, dare I say it, is the kind of yacht owner politicians mean when they have a pop at the wealthy. This book is for true travellers and adventurers.

My friend on his shrimping trawler had converted an old wooden shrimping trawler into a liveaboard passage maker thus probably saving a beautiful boat with heaps of character from the knackers yard. Whether it fulfilled all the requirements of a passage maker I cannot say, but you get my drift and certainly it was a travelling liveaboard.

If you are familiar with the old wooden RNLI lifeboats, from the 1960s and 70s, not open boats but closed motorboats in effect, quite a few of those are now liveaboards, again preserving a bit of our culture and nautical history. They're very strong and safe and clearly can make a home but they won't have the range to cross oceans. If you wanted to cross the channel and visit European rivers and canals there are worse bets, but they're not numerous or widely available.

From memory they were made of triple diagonal teak or mahogany. Planks laid at one angle, then another then another on top. They were incredibly strong and utilised the best hardwood, no wonder many survive. The reason I wouldn't touch a wooden yacht, as tempting as some are is maintenance.

Wood rots, even the best hardwood will rot eventually and you're asking it to live in water, salt water as a rule. The wood requires a certain amount of water, within it so to speak. It also needs paint and varnish to protect it. That's going to be a regular job. Take your wooden boat out of the water for a lengthy period and the wood starts to dry out, when that happens planks start to shrink and when you launch again it will be rather leaky.

Keep it in the water and pump it out periodically and the planks will swell again until it's once more watertight or very nearly watertight. A well constructed, well maintained wooden boat will have heaps of character and if it's the right size, shape and rig it'll go pretty much anywhere. Wood was largely superseded by fibreglass when it comes to yachts and so wooden boats tend to be older, 1960s and back as a general rule, so the previous maintenance really matters. Even if it is stunning in every respect, you'll want to keep it that way, and you want to liveaboard so forget throwing it at a professional boatyard every winter, you'll be living aboard whilst any maintenance is done and that's a consideration. I've lived on my boat whilst it was out of the water, it's not as romantic as living on it in the water. For one thing you have to climb down a ladder to go to the marina toilets every time that becomes necessary in daylight or not in daylight, or pee in a bottle to be emptied later.

When your boat is out of the water for cleaning, painting, maintenance and so on, life changes somewhat, no toilet facilities on board, nor shower, although you'll probably be in a marina rather than a boatyard, you'll also need to be agile enough to drag the shopping up a ladder.

When your boat is out of the water for maintenance, life takes on a whole new routine especially if you're doing the rubbing down and painting, anti fouling and so on yourself. Most marinas in the Mediterranean certainly still allow you to do all that, but a handful, and heaven forbid it catches on won't allow you to liveaboard if the boat is out of the water. Others insist you use their 'craftsmen' they control the prices you pay and doubtless get a kick back, you simply pay. So be careful where you choose to work on your boat if it's not an emergency and you have a choice. Yachtties like us talk to one another and no marina owner wants an empty marina, so choose wisely and all should go well with your overhauls.

It's just that wood requires more tender loving care than some other materials. Earlier we talked about how much money you should have left over after purchasing your boat and how much you might need to live on and by that I meant fuel, food, harbour dues, insurance and not a lot more, it wasn't to cover hire cars to go exploring inland or posh meals out. Take on a wooden boat and you should keep a good deal more in reserve and reckon on a rather larger income. If you can't manage that then wood, sadly is not for you. Even if the Griff Rhys Jonses will look down their noses.

That brings me on to steel, a steel boat being what I had. She was thirty years old when I purchased her in 2003. The hull was made of 6mm steel, so even if a full 1mm had rusted away she'd still have been immensely strong. Everyone knows that steel rusts and that putting it in salt water will accelerate the process, so why on earth would anyone buy a steel boat?

This is a deep fin keel that has hit a rock. It has a large lead weight encapsulated within it, which gives the yacht great stability and righting potential. However, imagine if instead of hitting a rock under the water, this boat had hit floating debris or a partially submerged container. The damage to the fibreglass hull, with no metal behind it would have been substantial, water would rush in and the heavy lead weight, which has been straining in a downward direction since birth, would start to win the argument. A catamaran, gets its stability from two widely spaced floats in effect. My previous prejudices against catamarans are not completely eliminated, but there's much to think about and this is a clear example of that. It also make you think about a steel boat!

Well all sorts of boats from tug boats to tankers, fishing boats to ocean liners are made of steel, it's strong, it works, and, which I think is important, rust is visible, it doesn't work away unseen like rot can with wood, it makes horrible brown stains that scare you into action. Very often a huge brown stain on your lovely white paintwork indicates a very, very small amount of actual rust.

A steel boat can graze a rock and be more or less unscathed; when I was still a bit green around the gills, on my first major voyage to the Baltic I twice scraped an underwater rock, I soon learned to be more careful, but the damage when I dived under the keel was quite hard to find and of no consequence. Had I hit a rock with a deep fin keel bolted to a fibreglass or wooden hull it might have been a very different story indeed.

You may or may not know, despite Robert Redford's slightly strange film on the subject, that every year many steel shipping containers are swept overboard from container ships that are stacked high and have the misfortune to run into a storm. Said containers are supposed to have a safety feature which should ensure they sink to the bottom of the ocean and don't become a hazard to shipping. The companies that routinely allow their containers to fall overboard are probably not the ones to take their other responsibilities too seriously either and in fact no one really knows just how many shipping containers are bobbing around on the sea.

Worse still many are partly or wholly submerged but very close to the surface. With perfect visibility, a flat sea, a good pair of eyes and not moving too fast you might spot one and avoid it. In heavy seas, or at night, or if it's hidden below the surface, or if you come upon it just as nature calls a collision becomes extremely likely. The corner of a shipping container will hole most yachts, but the yacht most likely to survive is a steel yacht.

So, you can see there really are a lot of pros to buying a steel yacht. A lot of really high quality steel boats have been built in the Netherlands down the years and it's a good place to search. Although I bought my yacht in Ireland she was designed and built in the Netherlands. I still have the original drawings, if I won the lottery I'd have a new one built with a few ideas of my own thrown in. As you can see I'm quite a fan, but there are real downsides to steel that we cannot ignore.

The shock, horror news is that most steel boats rust from the inside out. The outside is covered in layers of paint and anti fouling paint and should that get damaged and start to rust it shows and you can do something about it. There are chemical treatments widely available that will convert surface rust into a layer you can apply paint to. So far so good. The inside of your steel boat may well be covered in large part by insulating materials.

If it is not properly insulated, then you will truly freeze in winter and roast alive in a Mediterranean summer. That's the first con of steel, you're living in a can. Over the top of the insulation material someone has built storage compartments, the heads, the beds, the table, there are water tanks, fuel tanks, holding tanks, the cabin floor or sole as it is known, wooden panelling, the cooker and so on. In the engine bay you can probably shine a light straight on to the steel, but if you need to work on it down there, you'll find batteries, cables and wiring, a prop shaft, maybe an Eberspacher type heater and all sorts of obstacles besides just the engine.

Basically the problem is that steel boats rust from the inside and this time you can't see it without ripping things out, with the possible exception of the engine bay, but even there getting to the rust, cleaning it, treating and painting it can be a nightmare. You may be sceptical, why should a steel boat rust on the inside? The answer is that boats are often a bit damp inside, condensation can be an issue, a drip from the stern gland, a hatch cover that lets a little rain water in, even if it's only temporary and you fix it. Leaking plumbing, toilet problems and spillages, all these things can lead to interior rust, even if you never encounter a huge wave that gets a few gallons of sea water through your defences, which you will if you travel far enough. All is not lost however, if the strength of a steel boat appeals to you as it did to me.

The newer the boat the less material is likely to have been lost and the more likely it is to be constructed of corrosion resistant steel. There isn't a steel suitable for boat building that won't corrode at all but there are steels now that are very resistant. What about stainless steel I hear you ask, it is possible, but hugely expensive and stainless steel I'm advised becomes brittle after long exposure to salt water. I think if stainless steel was suitable we'd see a lot more of it around.

If you're looking at a steel boat append some questions to the list at the back of this book. What kind of steel was used in the construction and what gauge or thickness? Note that often the hull will be thicker steel than the decks. How is the boat insulated? How has the previous owner checked the condition? Was the steel simply painted inside or was it epoxied on the inside. I've only come across one steel boat on my travels epoxied inside and out but it was a lovely clean thing.

Steel boats can be surveyed using ultrasound which will tell you the thickness of the steel at a given point. A good surveyor will take hundreds of readings and give you a diagram showing the thickness of the steel. The first steel boat I had surveyed was instantly condemned by the surveyor as being too rusty on the inside. That was on the east coast of England. Unfortunately I couldn't persuade that surveyor to travel to Ireland for the sake of consistency and a fair comparison. The surveyor in Ireland proceeded to the full survey and ultrasound.

Knowing that my hull was originally constructed of 6mm steel and finding readings between 5.5mm and 5.9mm for the most part I figured if it had lost that amount in thirty years it should see me out and so it proved. Going back to the first boat the surveyor advised that the entire inside be taken out the steel needle gunned, any that was too thin replaced and then the whole thing treated and put back together. You can replace areas easily enough thanks to the invention of welding and that goes for damaged areas too so steel offers some flexibility in those terms.

A beautiful, large, steel sailing boat that would make a terrific liveaboard for a family, strong, spacious and able to sail, but too much for a solo and probably a little daunting for a couple, there's quite a variety of steel boats though.

The outside of a steel boat can be sand blasted to get back to bare metal if necessary, that's not possible inside, but a needle gun does much the same on the inside surface. Metal needles pound the face of the steel dislodging all the rust. The original vendor felt such a major restoration wasn't necessary and returned my deposit and we parted very amicably. If you fancy a project boat to do up before you liveaboard, bringing an old steel boat back to life might be right for you. Especially if you're young, fit, strong and don't mind hard dirty work. The advantage would be that you could really protect the inside of the steel as well as the outside.

You could keep a photographic record to reassure the next owner should you sell in the future, and of course you could design the new interior around your exact wants, but don't expect to start travelling for a few years, it's almost a new boat we're talking about now and you'd need to pick up the boat itself for a song to make the expense and work worthwhile.

Steel isn't the only metal used in the construction of boats. Your next option is aluminium, which like steel is very strong and can be welded. It doesn't rust either, so looks like we've cracked it. Sadly, that's not the case, aluminium can be welded, but it's more of a skilled art than welding steel, I guess that's a minor con, but things get worse. Con number two is that aluminium boats are expensive, very expensive size for size. So if you can afford it it's still a metal boat that won't rust, isn't it. Well that's true it won't rust, but aluminium can corrode, rust is sort of terracotta in colour a whitish powder forms on alloys when they corrode but the result is still a loss of material.

You may have heard about metals being more or less noble, there's a scale, gold for example is a noble metal, silver and steel less so and so it goes on. Brass, copper, bronze they all have different ratings and when used together strange things can happen. Different metals expand and contract at different rates causing stress but the real problems start when you add water. Oops, and especially a corrosive fluid like salt water. When you have dissimilar metals sitting in a bath of corrosive liquid you have a battery of sorts and electrolytic corrosion can eat away aluminium at an alarming rate.

Electricity, water and a collection of metals can stir up and create a few problems. If you plug your aluminium boat into shore power there's even more potential for problems. That's way you usually see an aluminium boat trailing a cable in the water in marinas and they don't like to be berthed next to a steel boat.

Steel boats are fitted with what are known as sacrificial anodes, these are chunks if ignoble alloy bolted to the hull to attract corrosion to themselves rather than to the steel. In fact fibreglass and wooden boats have them too to protect the metal parts and propellers. Yes, chunks of alloy to attract the corrosion and we're now discussing an all alloy boat. Except it isn't all alloy, the engine may have a cast steel block, the propshaft will be another grade of steel, the propeller another metal altogether, there will be stainless hose clips, electrical wires and goodness knows what else made of metal, sometimes items with their own electric motors within them, such as pumps and maybe winches.

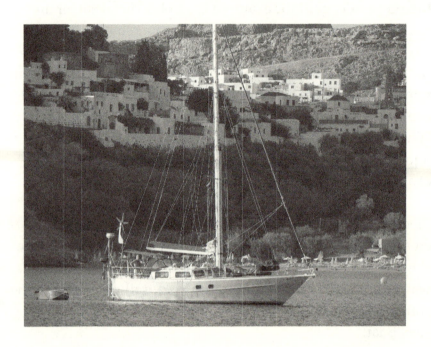

A large comfortable aluminium liveaboard, with plenty of weather protection, slab reefing for the mainsail AND steps up the mast, radar, wind generator, two foresails, one with roller reefing, there's a lot to like, if you can afford it and you know what you're taking on an aluminium boat could suit you well.

In theory if you dropped a penny into the bilge of you aluminium boat and there was salt water present the penny could happily corrode its way right through the hull leaving a nice little hole in its wake. However, I don't want to be alarmist about aluminium boats. The designers and builders know the problems and if you follow the instructions it won't be the huge issue I may have inferred it to be. It is a complication though and you will have to take care. For me the biggest downside to an aluminium boat is cost. If you can afford it, if you're aware of the potential issues and prepared to follow the rules an aluminium boat would make a lovely blue water travelling liveaboard.

That brings us on to fibreglass. People refer to them as plastic boats or tupperware, especially some of the classic wooden, blue blazer types. Chances are my next boat will be fibreglass it might be steel, but one of those two. You'd think that a fibreglass boat would be impervious to water, end of story. Sadly even this material is not perfect. Your enemy if you have a fibreglass boat is something called osmosis. Osmosis is something that goes on at the molecular level, it's not something you can really see with the naked eye until blisters form. Basically individual water molecules eventually weedle their way between the molecules of the gel coat.

One way of extending the life of a fibreglass boat is to dry it out every winter. If you're a liveaboard you don't really want to be living aboard a boat out of water. Most of us have done it at some time and this lifestyle will involve some sacrifices to set against having the world and the sunrise and the whales and dolphins to yourself.

Osmosis is another of those subjects that gets talked about in marina bars all over the world. Some take it very seriously, others think it's merely cosmetic. I'm in the take it seriously camp and get it sorted but don't let it keep you awake at night. I took one of my training courses on a fibreglass boat that was about seven years old and had never been dried out. I'm not a surveyor but I feel that drying it out every year probably isn't essential and when you do take it out for anti fouling give it a short break of a couple of months if you can.

I heard a yachtie discussing osmosis with a surveyor in Turkey, the yachtsman said something like 'oh come on, no one has ever died because of osmosis'. The surveyor retorted that 'boats get lost all the time and we don't necessarily know if they broke up or why and that even if you're right chances are someone will one day'. Different views but if I had a fibreglass boat and I knew there was osmosis I'd want to nip it in the bud.

This is the Nicholson 38 I mad an offer on, more space than the boat I ended up with and more luxurious too, whilst still having a wheelhouse and radar and the ketch rig I prefer. The spool on the handrail aft is a Scandinavian Ankoralina, a webbing line on a spool that's more or less essential if you visit Sweden and Scandinavian locations as they have a mooring system in marinas which requires picking up a buoy and attaching said line. I had to buy one. There are special boathooks that help you pick up moorings you'll find them in chandleries and at boat shows, not essential but very helpful, especially solo. The Ankoralina can have a purpose made stainless hook that will snap on to a ring on the buoy, also good to have. The only thing I would have regretted had the purchase of this boat succeeded was the wooden decks, hugely expensive to replace, need to be kept wet regularly so the wood doesn't shrink in sunny climes and will burn the soles of your feet if you go barefoot in hot places.

I looked at a Nicholson 38 when I was shopping for my boat, a surveyor later told me I should have got it, he loved them and it is a fabulous boat. When I had it surveyed the surveyor found both a small crack in the hull and some osmosis. The Nic was at the absolute top of my budget so we costed the repair and to have the entire gel coat replaced, which would really have made the hull like new. The vendor wouldn't accept an offer reduced by the cost of the work so I bought the boat in Ireland. Within a week the vendor of the Nicholson came back and said he'd accept my reduced offer.

He was too late and arguably we both lost out although I loved my steel boat, sailed thousands and thousands of miles, learned, made mistakes and she kept me safe, so no complaints.

I've really only talked about the problems of fibreglass but the advantages are many. So many fibreglass boats have been built that you'll almost certainly find one that is the size you want, the hull type you want, the rig you want and with the features and equipment you want. At the time of writing it's a buyers market, but because of the popularity of fibreglass boats they probably depreciate less than the others we've discussed or at the least sell more easily should you move on.

This is a typical modern fibreglass yacht, the Ford Fiesta of the boat world in my view, does everything quite well, comfortable and practical to live on especially if you're happy with an open cockpit. Every marina has people who know them and how to work on them. The standing rigging is standard so not too onerous to replace every ten years. It's worth consideration, there are lots of them so bargains are available, but fibreglass boats don't only come in this configuration.

So many fibreglass boats are in effect mass produced boats the parts are readily available and boatyards are likely to have engineers and workmen and women who know their way around the major brand boats. Most fibreglass boats have alloy masts and spars rather than wooden masts and spars, all these things help to make the maintenance more reasonable. Insurance companies want the standing rigging changed every ten years these days. Standard boat, standard rigging and people who know how to do it, much simpler than a unique boat like mine.

Fibreglass boats have of course evolved and you'll hear bar room debate about how thin the fibreglass is on new boats, on some you can even see the sun through the side of the boat on occasion and that's not reassuring. My friend the carpenter who does boat interiors is very scathing about certain new boats from certain brands. I don't want him or me to face legal action so I won't name manufacturers. He reckons they're so lightly built that after five to ten years of active sailing the stresses will cause the bulkheads to start pulling away form the hull.

I can't confirm or deny this, if the boat was very cheap when new and appears lightly built, talk to your surveyor. With production boats he will have seen a few and he'll know. Follow his professional advice. My budget tends to restrict me to slightly older boats anyway, although as I've said there are some unbelievable deals at this particular time.

This is a Nauticat 38 clearly not a catamaran as you might think from the name. It won't sail as fast or as close to the wind as the Bavaria pictured previously, the 34 foot variant can't really be considered anything other than a motor sailer, but this one is very roomy, very comfortable, great wheelhouse and you can have outside steering too. Heavily constructed in Scandinavia the Nauticat is a great liveaboard and Nauticat have different keel options available on some models, so although a motor sailer not all of them should be written off in terms of sailing qualities.

An older fibreglass boat wouldn't scare me at all if it got a good survey, or if the gel coat was renewed. Early fibreglass boats were very heavily built precisely because no one knew how this new material would hold up in use on the high seas. They got lighter simply because it held up so very well. Whether they've got too light now is debatable and of course the actual materials used have improved with experience and new technologies. Good survey and a discussion with your surveyor about the type and he'll set you right.

Fibreglass is easy to keep clean and white fibreglass reflects the sun. Try not to get one with teak decks laid on top of the fibreglass decks. A bit of wood inside, or in the cockpit or wheelhouse, lovely, to walk on in a hot climate with bare feet, agony, to replace costly and it can trap sea water too, although a relatively small consideration it adds weight, as well as absorbing heat that makes the boat hotter to live in. White is bright, in my view.

The final con to fibreglass is its fragility compared with steel, aluminium or ferro cement, should you hit a rock, which you should be able to avoid, or a shipping container or other debris, or even suffer an attack by whales which has been known and which are things it's much harder to avoid then fibreglass could be more easily holed. Remember early ones we're built tougher than later ones. The odds on hitting a container or being attacked by whales are long odds, it's a calculated risk and it's your calculation. This book is to focus your mind on the many considerations.

This ferro cement yacht belongs to a friend who lived aboard for years, here we are on the Guadilquivir river near Seville. His boat was beautifully constructed, but insurance was a difficulty as you can't see what's going on within the material. Wooden masts add to the maintenance and the gaff rig is heavy but if you're a real man... or tough lady of course. The bowsprit is retractable, very handy in marinas. Note the wind generator necessary for real independence and the sunshade, something you'll want to rig up on any kind of yacht when visiting hotter climates than the UK. The traditional ratlines make getting up the mast quite easy.

The final option is ferro cement or reinforced concrete if you will. There was a craze for these, build one in your back garden then sail off around the world. Lots of people bought into the idea and quite a few were home built, others never got finished and a few were built by people who really knew what they were doing. My friend Terry has one I wouldn't take one if it was given to me, but I have to say that Terry's boat was built by a skilled engineer and since Terry finished the project it became a thing of beauty. Terry showed me behind the panels and in the bilges, the workmanship and the finish and attention to detail in places most people will never see is impressive. It is in my view likely to be the exception that proves the rule however.

Reinforced concrete is basically steel reinforcing rods set in concrete or cement. Ferro boats were a basket work of steel rods set into concrete. Terry told me he'd seen one that had fallen off a low loader on the motorway, it just bounced he said, second in strength only to a steel boat. That may be so, but many were built by amateurs and it's very hard to know if you've got a good one. If the steel was rusting already when the concrete was applied, if water has got in where it shouldn't those steel rods will rust and the integrity of the thing is lost.

We've seen or heard about bridge disasters caused by the same kind of fault but this is meant to live in salt water all its life, not merely sit in the rain. It does seem to me that now we have corrosion resistant steel and better cement and concrete that maybe today the time is right for ferro boats to make a comeback, but it's not happening so there are only old ones out there.

This is not the hull of a ferro cement boat, it's actually a storm damaged pontoon at a marina in Turkey. However the construction is similar. Where the concrete has been damaged by the clashing of pontoons in the storm the steel reinforcing rods have been revealed, what's left of them that is, prior to the breakage it looked like the section on the right and that's the difficulty with ferro cement boats in a nutshell.

They're cheap, very cheap because people don't trust them and insurance companies will only provide third party cover. You cannot adequately survey them. Ultrasound won't do it. If there are rust streaks down the hull you know the steel rods are rusting, cracks, even worse, but if everything looks perfect it may not be.

The only way to check then is to chip some concrete away until you find a rod or rods and inspect them. OK they're fine, six inches away or ten feet away, or on the opposite side the thing may be about to crumble away, you can't make hundreds of holes in it. Basically the hull cannot be surveyed, it was probably built by an amateur, its best days are probably behind it and you can't insure it adequately, which is why, in my opinion it's a non starter, unless they start making them professionally with better modern materials. Which someone probably should.

My own conclusion is that I personally would only buy a fibreglass or a steel yacht, I won't repeat everything above it's probably plain why I feel that way. If I was wealthy I'd love a classy wooden classic that someone else would maintain and I'd take the plaudits, but that's not me. If I was wealthy I might consider an aluminium boat, strong, light modern, but I think I'd always be a bit worried about corrosion, although cost is the major barrier for me. However poor I might be I wouldn't trust my life to an old ferro boat, so that leaves just steel and fibreglass. I regard steel as safer if it's a good one, fibreglass is very practical, widely available, easy to maintain (relatively), holds it's value better if any boat is going to, I could live with either.

If you're a novice do consider steel, but whatever it's made of try not to hit anything or run aground!

Now lets consider the shape and design of the thing.

CHAPTER 5
HULL DESIGN

Now we are going to discuss the shape of your boat and in particular the type of keel it might have. The combination of hull shape and keel type will have a bearing for any given overall length on things such as interior space, much prized by liveaboards, stability, sailing performance, not just speed but the boat's ability to point up, or sail to windward. I will explain shortly.

The hull and keel combination will also have a great bearing on the boat's draft or depth. Rivers tend to transport silt down to the sea and where it meets with the sea and tides the river frequently builds what is known as a sand bar at the entrance to the river. If it's an important commercial river the authorities will often maintain a dredged channel, but that isn't always the case, even some marinas silt up so a shallow draft opens up a greater diversity of options to stop and visit places.

My boat wasn't the greatest in terms of sailing performance, but she was adequate to my needs.

A deep fin keel will generally speaking offer greater stability in mid Atlantic (although I was incredibly impressed with the stability of my shallow long keeled boat, even in a mid Atlantic storm) but a deep keel won't let you into many a small Greek island. The good news is, that although everything in boat design is a compromise or trade off, there are some areas where you can have your cake and eat it if there are certain other features or aspects you can live without. For example my boat did not sail at all well to windward, but she was both shallow draft and very stable in an Atlantic storm, and she was spacious for a 35 footer to boot!

So, pointing up or sailing to windward. I grew up racing sailing dinghies on a lake in Epping Forest and when you learn something at a young age it tends to stick. I knew these things before I bought a yacht. If you don't understand how sails work I would recommend you take one of the excellent RYA (Royal Yachting Association) dinghy sailing courses.

A typical fin keel

Bilge keels allow a boat to stand on the ground, beach, seabed....

This boat has a drop keel and also a bow thruster, the hole beneath the waterline near the bow is actually a tunnel with a propeller inside to aid manoeuvring.

Sailing to windward means sailing against the wind. Old square riggers could barely do this, with modern sails that run almost along the centre line of the boat ie fore and aft and with modern keel design some boats can sail almost directly into wind, not quite of course there has to be some angle if you point directly into wind your sails will merely flap. This is called being in irons, because it can be hard to get out of it.

The closer your boat will sail to the wind the fewer tacks you will have to make to progress against the wind. There is an aerodynamic effect, the sail acting a bit like the aerofoil section of an aircraft wing. However, for simplicity think about a slippery bar of soap slightly curved from use, grip it tightly on both sides and it may well slip sideways out of your grasp.

A deep fin keel will give you this kind of performance and enable you to sail close to the wind, which is more useful. These guys are racers, not liveaboards and big sails like these are far more manageable mob handed.

The keel of your boat opposes sideways motion, the sail is trying to push the boat sideways against the keel, it can't do it, but because the boat has a pointy front end it can slip forwards, like the bar of soap. There's more to it than that given aerodynamics and it gets more complicated still, unsurprisingly, if the keel is not terribly efficient it will still slip sideways a little. This is called leeway, your bow may be pointed where you want to go but it doesn't represent the direction of travel over the ground, even if it looks like you're sailing well to windward. Your gps will reveal the truth about your true direction of travel!

Nonetheless the bar of soap analogy gives you some idea how it works and dinghy sailing will increase your understanding a hundredfold and you'll also learn about luffing up, beam and broad reaches, running before the wind, kicking straps, gybing and much more that this book won't be covering. If you know what gybing is, my boat had a gybe controller to protect the mast and rigging from the shock of an accidental or uncontrolled gybe. I wouldn't want to live without one now. It's on the list of questions to ask at the end of the book.

My boat would barely progress against the wind at all, especially if there were waves to knock the bow off. With the right wind, a calm sea and with the use of the slot effect from two foresails I could make a little progress but it was terribly slow, you wouldn't make twenty miles up the coast in a day with the wind against you. In that instance my options were to motor against the wind which can be slow and costly although not as slow as trying to sail, or wait for the wind to change. Which is what I normally did. I figured on any given day I had a choice of three directions in effect and if I wanted the other one I'd wait, but not everyone wants to be that patient or philosophical, so you may want a boat that does sail well or even very well to windward. Personally I wouldn't make it a top priority for this lifestyle though.

If you look at a modern yacht designed with sailing performance or racing in mind she'll look fast often beamiest or widest behind the centre of the boat with a long narrowing line all the way to the pointy bit. Usually such boats will have a deep fin keel, often with a weight at the bottom. Although many high performance mono hulls sail very fast whilst heeled over a lot of boats cut through the water best when more or less upright.

You, are not looking for ultimate performance if your boat is wider for longer, you'll have heaps more interior space for the same length and given you want to live on board, all year, along with all your clothes and some books and probably music and other diversions, space matters. Not to mention provisioning for the longer voyages, carrying fresh drinking water and so on. Look for the less racy style of boat, it doesn't mean it won't sail to windward.

Most yachts have an open cockpit at the stern, some have a central cockpit and some again have a wheelhouse. If you like being outside come rain, come shine, an open cockpit is fine, many have spray dodgers and folding screens to protect you from the worst of the spray and waves, some have biminis to provide shade from the hot sun. However the sun can still burn even when it's not at its zenith and a bit of cloth above you isn't always enough.

I loved my wheelhouse which was wooden for half its length with a canopy behind with opening windows to let the breeze in but still keep you out of the sun. Skin cancer is just as deadly as drowning. In cold, stormy, wet weather a cockpit can be a miserable place. When you are travelling, even if you employ an autopilot or self steering gear for much of the time you'll still be on watch. Given the amount of time you'll spend in the cockpit or wheelhouse, make sure it offers good comfort and protection. It's also where you'll host your parties! As a final thought, when boats are riding waves there's a point at which they tend to pivot, it's usually aft of centre.

If you go up to the bow in rough weather you'll find it rises and falls much more than your centre cockpit which isn't actually central but is a little behind centre and usually about where the pivot point is ie the least uncomfortable place. The stern will still be more comfortable than the bow and cockpits are fine for the hardy, but a centre cockpit, better yet one covered in a wheelhouse suits me fine. I used my separate aft cabin as a guest room and I slept in the bow when in harbour or at anchor, but if I needed a cat nap at sea I used the aft cabin, much more comfortable on the open sea and I could jump up into the wheelhouse, where all the controls were and where all the running rigging terminated, in an instant if it seemed necessary.

Some boats have what is known as a 'canoe stern' in other words it has a pointy bit at each end, although the stern will not be as pointy as the bow, more rounded. I'm told that a canoe stern breaks a following sea. It seems to me that a canoe stern boat might be very slightly faster than the same boat would be if it stayed wide and had a big square transom like mine. My large rear cabin with two single beds was very useful though, for storage, for guests and for catnaps at sea. The issue of sailing solo and maintaining a watch is a big subject in it's own right and not part of the remit of this book. I will mention that some radar systems have an audible alarm, mine did and if you're looking at a boat with radar you should ask about that. Back to the canoe stern however, my boat with a large, high square stern coped well, in my view, running before a hurricane force Atlantic storm. I cannot say if it would or wouldn't have been easier with a canoe stern. If the boat you're looking at has enough room for your needs and a canoe stern I certainly wouldn't view that as a negative.

This is what's meant by a canoe stern, lovely cutter ketch rigged liveaboard too.

Now to keels; your choices of keel are pretty much as follows deep fin keel, with or without a bulb or weight at the bottom. Wing keel which is basically a fin keel with two slightly downward angled wings on each side at the bottom. One can mentally visualise how these might add to stability when the boat is heeled over and the fin itself has become far from vertical. I've never sailed one but I'm told they perform well.

Next you have bilge keels, normally this means two fins, one on each side pointing down and away from each other slightly. See the various pictures provided.

Here we have the propeller and rudder of a long keel Formosa Yacht. As on my boat, the rudder and propeller are very well protected by the keel. Despite the appearance of wooden planking the Formosa is actually fibreglass and a very comfortable, large liveaboard into the bargain.

Here you can see virtually the entire keel of the Formosa.

Bilge keels can be long and not very deep but these usually accompany a long keel. A long keeled boat is what I had. The bow is perforce narrow and somewhat slab-sided so like a keel it resists sideways motion to some extent, as the hull widens and flattens out it normally rises gradually towards the transom or stern of the boat but the long keel takes its line straight back, more or less, from the lowest part of the bow, allowing for an ever increasing vertical section or keel along the centreline of the boat ending with the propeller and rudder.

The final option, if we exclude catamarans is a lifting or drop keel, whichever description you prefer, it's the same thing. A lifting keel is effectively a fin keel that can be lowered or winched up, generally into a vertical, central cavity in the main cabin which then becomes the support for the dining table. Good use of space on a boat is vital.

This lovely sleek yet spacious catamaran is what's known as a daggerboard cat you can see the raised daggerboard on this the windward side, just behind the mast from this angle. I like this design, good sailing performance, but very shallow draft and all the other advantages of a catamaran.

Catamarans can have a long keel under each hull, a different profile than that described above, but still a long keel, or a catamaran can be what's known as a daggerboard cat, it has daggerboards or keels that slide up and down much as you'll find on many dinghies. A catamaran relies for its stability on having two floats, one on each side in effect but in order to sail well, it, like any other yacht needs something to resist sideways motion.

Just as all the different materials that your boat might be made of have their pros and cons, so do each of these keels so let's look at them individually.

Your fin keel will outperform all others as a rule of thumb in terms of sailing performance. Westerly offered at least one yacht where owners could specify a fin keel or bilge keels making like for like comparison a possibility. I'm lumping together wing keels, straightforward fin keels and fins with a weight at the bottom. A fin keel with a weight at the bottom will make for a very stable sailing boat, and any fin keel boat is likely to have reasonable ability to sail to windward. So what are the cons?

That fin heading straight down makes your yacht one of the deeper yachts around, making it more difficult to cross sandbars and barring you from shallow harbours. If you should sail your keel straight into a partially submerged rock the results could be catastrophic. If you should run aground when the tide is falling that too could prove catastrophic. If you've ever seen little indentations on a dance floor made by stiletto shoes you'll appreciate it's because the wight is concentrated in a small area. If you ask your boat to take its weight on the narrow fin keel, well, it should be designed to take it but bounce it up and down on the waves and keep hitting it on the sea floor and it might pop through and join you in the cabin.

If the tide falls sufficiently your boat will simply topple over, that might break it open, but if it doesn't it could be touch and go whether, lying on its side, it refloats or fills with water when the tide comes up again. If the sailing performance of a deep fin keel matters that much to you, don't make mistakes. If you're a novice I'd give it a miss. I've seen a famous ocean racer with a deep fin keel run aground in front of me when I was anchored in Ibiza. One would imagine it had an experienced crew, anyone can make a mistake. I watched the battle to get her out of danger with great interest for several hours.

One final thought if your fin keel has a bloomin' great weight at the bottom to help keep the yacht upright and sailing fast what will that weight do if you hit a container and get holed – it'll pull you downwards and help you sink is what it'll do. A fin keel might mark you out as a serious sailor, but it wouldn't be my first choice. Fin keeled boats usually have a deep fin shaped rudder or rudders and between the keel and the rudder the propshaft protrudes with the propeller at the end. Your rudder and propeller are less vulnerable than your keel, but they have far less protection than on a long keel boat for example.

After deep fin keels the next option is bilge keels. Since you now have two keels they don't need to be as deep, or have appendages, win number one. Sailing performance is likely to be slightly less and you'll have more drag, but it won't be horribly deficient and many bilge keeled boats sail very well. I haven't sailed a fin keeled boat with a wing, but I have sailed, fin, bilge and long keeled boats and bilge keeled boats can as I said sail very well. I would consider this option.

Not only is your draft reduced but bilge keeled boats are designed to stand up, on the sea bed, on a trailer, in a marina. If you do get caught out by a falling tide, even though you shouldn't, then if it's a sandy bottom your boat will stand there just fine. You may want to take it close to shore in a sandy anchorage at high tide on purpose and deliberately stand it up as the tide falls so you can inspect the hull and the anodes and antifouling, it's a very practical proposition and you should be able to sail to windward too.

When this deep fin keel ocean racer ran aground in Menorca it was possible to get her going again by using a powerful RIB to tilt her over and get the keel free. It took several hours and several attempts mind. This won't work with two bilge keels as one side would dig deeper in as the other became free.

When the Ocean Racer Assa Abloy ran aground in Ibiza a motorboat eventually took her halyard and motored away sideways pulling the top of the mast over and heeling the boat, this finally lifted the central fin keel off the seabed and the boat could be moved to deeper water. If you accidentally run aground with your bilge keeled boat, heeling her over will free one side but dig the other side in deeper, in short it won't work, but that's a minor consideration, if you're in tidal water you should be safe enough until you float off at some stage. If you're not in a tidal area you'll need help.

The next keel design is long keel. Even shallower draft than bilge keels, now you can get in almost anywhere. Furthermore your long keel is very robust, especially on a steel boat but even on a wooden or fibreglass boat the shape is inherently strong and it's not just bolted on either. A long keel automatically offers greater protection to the propeller and rudder than other keel designs, another win. My long keel boat could take the ground as with a bilge keeled boat in a harbour that dried out with the falling tide, like some on the east coast of Britain. It might lean over a bit but it wouldn't fall and would usually make a little nest for itself in the mud and sit there quite happy and vertical.

My own long keel is visible in this photograph from Kusadasi, you can see the excellent protection afforded the rudder and propeller, but there's less keel to resist sideways movement, especially at the front, when compared with the Formosa pictured previously.

Not all long keeled boats perform the same, my sailing to windward performance was woeful and if I'd had more money I'd have considered welding some bilge keels on her, long and not terribly deep, but if they went far enough forwards they might have held the bow on course better and reduced leeway. I'll never know but I've seen long keeled boats with long bilge keels on each side that don't increase the draft at all but probably enhance the sailing performance.

A boat with three keels in effect should also take the ground well and spread the load. What I would say about long keels is that you can't take either sailing performance or the ability to take the ground for granted. They vary too much. Talk to the vendor, talk to the surveyor and get a sea trial, you need these questions answered to help you make a decision that's right for you. Just looking at the variety of shapes available I'm sure there are long keeled boats around that would trounce mine in terms of pointing up.

A finger pontoon is a very narrow pontoon jutting out at right angles from the main pontoon, makes life very easy but most Mediterranean marinas don't have them, instead a marinero in a rib will pass you an oft times mollusc encrusted dirty line to attach to your stern if you've gone bows to or vice versa. They can fit more boats in that way, but you have to be very careful entering and leaving as you'll be cheek by jowl with your neighbour. My boat didn't steer well in reverse, nor did it have a bow thruster but I developed strategies to cope. This picture is typical of a Mediterranean marina, note most boats have a passerelle to make it easier to get on and off.

Here you see the Scandinavian marina mooring system with an Ankoralina attached to a buoy and all boats bows to. Cleaner than the Mediterranean system and easier too. It offers greater privacy as well, since most boats have the entrance to the main cabin at the rear. Many Scandinavian boats come with a folding ladder built on to the bow to make this system even more practical.

One thing most owners of long keeled boats seem to agree on is that they don't steer well in reverse. Sounds trivial but it isn't all that trivial. In Britain most marinas have finger pontoons you either motor in or reverse in. In Europe most marinas expect you to moor bows to or stern to and many, probably the majority, have a line attached to the sea bed that you take to your stern if you've gone bows to. There's no finger pontoon between you and your neighbour.

When you reverse out, you will not be wanting to hit the boats around you, it's costly and embarrassing, not that I've done it thankfully. Your propeller turns, naturally, and although the blades are angled to push water forwards or back depending what gear you're in, imagine for a moment that it's also a kind of paddle wheel. There is a phenomenon known as prop walk, it wants to paddle off to the side it's turning towards and that will pull the stern around.

Some walk one way in reverse, some the other, you'll get to know which. It means turning one way in reverse is a doddle, the other way is next to impossible as the rudder is fighting the prop walk. What I did was try and enter a slot which would require me to back out the easy way. So I planned for departure when I arrived. Often a marina will tell you which is your spot or there may only be one space left. In instances where I had to turn the wrong way in order to leave I'd give a powerful burst of reverse to get it moving and get into neutral as soon as possible to then be able to steer, but with the wrong wind direction, you really would need a marinero to help, preferably one in an inflatable with an outboard so he can push your bow or stern around as required.

These days many boats have bow thrusters, that is a propeller mounted in a tunnel across the bow, to push it in either direction when manoeuvring. Very useful, although if you're sufficiently skilled you won't need it very often. Fin and regular bilge keeled boats seem to be able to cope with prop walk better than long keeled boats for some reason. Nonetheless I like long keeled boats. Sailing to windward was my big deficiency but prop walk was a small problem overall and the protection afforded to my rudder and propeller, and my shallow draft were a godsend. Find one that sails well and you've really got it all.

I'm not going to say much about lee boards which are those rounded off triangular plates you see on the sides of old sailing barges. They swing down from the top of the triangle and back up again, so are a type of lifting keel I suppose and a sailing barge would make a great and spacious liveaboard, if you're wealthy enough to cope with the maintenance of an old wooden classic. You wouldn't cross oceans in one though and you'd need a crew for even short sailing trips, so they fall outside the remit of this book.

Yachts with lifting keels are a different matter. The aforementioned MacGregor has one so do aluminium Ovnis and fibreglass Southerlys and some other brands. Some like the MacGregor will have lifting rudders and will be able to take the ground, if it's soft but don't bank on it, there's always the propeller to look after, the Macgregor has an outboard motor that can be tilted up, larger boats don't.

This Dutch barge and an Ovni with a lifting keel accompanied me through the Dutch canals. My boat was the least roomy and the deepest of the three!

Lifting keel boats have always struck me as a great idea. I went through the Dutch canals with some friends. Two of my friends were French and had an Ovni, the other family was Dutch and had a barge with lee boards. Although my boat was shorter than the Ovni and less spacious than the barge, I was the deepest of the three! Sufficiently shallow though which is what matters.

A lifting keel boat gives you the sailing performance and stability of a fin keel and a draft that's almost as shallow as a catamaran. If you hit a rock, with luck the keel will fold up rather than disintegrate or come off. If you're sailing downwind and you don't need so much keel to resist sideways movement you can raise it part way. To my way of thinking there's only one downside to a lifting keel and that's complication. Even that wouldn't be an issue were it not for sealife.

I'd recommend coppercoat as an antifouling, but whatever you use things will try and colonise your boat. They love small spaces, chains and just about anything they can get a purchase on so the space your keel retracts into is very inviting. That's the main con from where I see it, more maintenance, but from every other angle they look good to me.

Catamarans are a whole new subject, as I said before I had a considerable prejudice against them. In a sudden squall a monohull will heel over and spill wind while you get things sorted. A catamaran might break it's mast or worse flip over. In fact catamarans tend to have much stronger rigging. Pull up the daggerboards if you have a daggerboard cat and the whole can slip sideways, if necessary while you deal with the sails. I looked at those two pointy bits with nothing but a trampoline between them and thought about them pointing down a wave and then digging in like two spears.

I've seen damaged catamarans and it's not pretty, but as with everything it's not simple. After talking at length to a catamaran designer I can appreciate they have many good points too. I now like the idea of a daggerboard catamaran one with deck at the front and shaped to give lift between the hulls if necessary. A few years ago I was told there was a race in the southern hemisphere where an unexpected major storm prompted the organisers to airlift the crews from the catamarans. After the storm all the catamarans were located, all afloat and all the right way up!

There are catamarans that were designed as motorboats and others have had the mast removed by owners not intending to sail, this one appears to have been dismasted though, look closely and you'll see the attachment points for rigging and on the far side the handrail is damaged, possibly where the mast came down. I've seen a catamaran with worse damage, but only these two in ten years. I've also seen a monohull with a broken mast, so I haven't written catamarans off.

A deep fin keeled monohull with a large weight on the keel will be dragged downward by that weight if the hull is holed. Not so with a lightweight catamaran sitting virtually on top of the water, much more time to try and save the boat and probably one hull still fully buoyant.

In a real crisis the catamaran owner can probably stay with his disabled boat, the monohull that's gone to the bottom is truly gone. The owner may be in a life raft but for survival the catamaran that's still partially afloat has better odds. It's easier to spot from the air than a liferaft. It may still have a working radio, there may still be access to food and pure water. Don't abandon your boat until you have to climb upwards into the liferaft.

To happier things however. As mentioned before, your catamaran owner can go into very shallow places, anchor close to shore where there is more shelter. He can take the ground, he has loads of living and storage space. Catamarans can be quite fast and although not all, many will point well to windward. I should think all head up better than my boat and a daggerboard cat should be pretty good.

If you can find a good catamaran at a price you can afford and if you can afford the higher marina costs, then potentially you've got a great blue water, travelling boat gypsy liveaboard. I've met several families or couples doing it and several had crossed oceans. My anti catamaran prejudice is now a thing of the past.

In conclusion I personally would buy a boat of any keel design now that I have many years of experience, but even so a fin keel would be my last choice, everything else about the boat would have to be screaming buy me. If you're a novice I'd avoid it, but it's a calculated risk, up to you. The main downside for me is draft, I want to be able to get into interesting places and up rivers. Bilge keels if shallow enough and if the boat sailed well enough and was stable, fine by me.

Long keel again I know I can live with and if it could take the ground and sail up wind a bit better than the last one I'd be in clover. Lifting keel or catamaran, absolutely if the right one came along at the right price, absolutely. I've tried to explain the pros and cons in layman's terms. I hope it makes sense to you and will help you decide when you start looking at boats. The vendor of a deep fin keel boat will probably rave about how well it sails but there's more than that at stake.

Now that we've looked at what's under the water, lets go up top and discuss the rig.

CHAPTER 6
THE RIG

There are two yachts in this picture, racing with Spinnakers, look closely and you'll see the one in the background is having something of a problem. A Spinnaker or variant thereof is not something I consider important for the travelling liveaboard gypsy, especially one on his or her own, unnecessary complication, chill out and travel slowly, works fine for me. Spinnakers can be a handful and very powerful.

The majority of yachts you'll see advertised for sale, will be what's known as Sloops or Sloop rigged. A Sloop has one mast, a main sail called a mainsail unsurprisingly and a fore sail or foresail, these come in different sizes and have different names. They come under the broad heading of jibs, but you can have a Storm Jib, which is very small, a Staysail a bit bigger and a Genoa which is pretty big and comes back far enough to overlap the mainsail. For racing a Sloop may carry a Spinnaker which is like a large balloon shaped sail that spreads out low, balloons upwards and terminates in a point at the masthead. To complicate matters further there are variations known as Gennakers, part Genoa, part Spinnaker and Running Sails.

This is a modern sloop, she'll sail well, even in light winds as here, but with two large sails she can be a bit of a handful in a sudden squall with all sail up. Especially solo.

The good news is that as a solo sailor, not racing you really can do without Spinnakers and Gennakers, a running sail, or cruising chute might be useful on occasion, but I probably wouldn't bother. The fewer the hands on board the simpler you want to make life in my view. Most sloops sail very well, modern yacht design really is very good, but there are drawbacks. Goodness, here we go again, everything is a compromise.

I suspect that at least part of the reason so many Sloops are built is that a boat with just one mast is cheaper to build, and has less rigging too, plus the manufacturer can point to great speed and performance, because masts tend to be tall and sails large. A large sail generates a lot of power, but it's also a big handful if you don't reef it down in time or get caught out.

Reefing a sail is a way of making it smaller to cope with increasing wind strengths, the stronger the wind, not unnaturally the smaller the sail area you need and of course in theory, too much sail and too much wind could lead to a capsize, although it's rare with modern monohulls that are designed with huge safety margins and righting properties and which spill wind as they heel over.

Nonetheless, you don't want to be reefing your mainsail with the boat stood on its ear, I know I've done it after leaving someone else on watch who didn't want to wake me just because the wind was getting up a bit!

There are several ways of reefing a mainsail. The traditional way is called slab reefing. Usually the sail has two or three rows of grommets and ties, you lower the sail the desired amount flaking, or folding it neatly in slabs either side of the boom and tie it down in place. Normally you'll turn into wind to achieve this but this isn't a how to sail book I'm simply trying to identify the different systems you might be faced with so you can think about which boat to buy.

Get the vendor to show you how the reefing works, and take some RYA training and ask questions about these things, the boat you do your training on will have just one type of reefing naturally, so don't be afraid to ask about the others, maybe the school has access to other boats and can show you.

There are lines called lazy jacks which should prevent the sail going all over the place as you lower it and some modern boats have a sail bag attached to the boom to gather it up. Many sails have battens or stiffeners in them to help them achieve the most effective shape in use. Slab reefing deals well with the battens as you can fold them in without bending or damaging them as you reef the sail.

The second common form of reefing is called in mast furling. The mast looks deeper fore and aft than a normal mast because it has a container housing a vertical roller. When you look at a boat with in mast furling it looks like it doesn't have a sail at all until you notice a small triangle of something, usually blue, sticking out of the mast, just above the boom with ropes attached. So, the sail itself is neatly rolled up in the mast. Pull on the appropriate line and out it rolls, as much or as little of it as you want, pull on another line and in it rolls once more. A hugely variable size of sail and oh so easy. The little blue triangle that pokes out of the mast is the corner of the sail, protected on either side from the sun by replaceable sacrificial canvas that just happens to be blue most of the time.

This yacht has entered harbour with a ripped Genoa, but being in the open, most of it has rolled away. Look closely and you'll see it also has in mast furling for the mainsail which has to pass through a narrow slot. Had the mainsail ripped then the in mast furling would have been a real liability.

No trying to fold and tie a powerful flapping sail, no climbing on the wheelhouse roof if you have one, trying not to step on the solar panels or navigation lights, or fall off as the boat pitches in the waves. Great, in mast furling it is then. Vendors will rave about it and list it as a selling point. I've seen just two boats in difficulty due to in mast furling in ten years at sea, but it's enough to put me right off.

Like most things they're great when they work. When things get a bit rough the sail, flapping as you roll it away may crease and not roll up cleanly and if it doesn't roll neatly it may fill the available space before it's all in. However, the real fun starts if you get a tear in the sail. It's true that when in the mast the sail is very, very well protected from the sun, but sails wear out eventually even so and even a new sail could burst a seam in extremis, especially if somewhere aloft it's been rubbing a bit as you pull it in and out.

A torn sail will not roll neatly away, it will self destruct, damaging itself and possibly the mast and rigging, not to mention your wallet as it does so. I saw a yacht with in mast furling sailing this way and that in an anchorage in Greece trying to deal with a torn sail and the in mast furling. In Licata, southern Sicily an elderly French gentleman came in with a sail he couldn't put away. I went up his mast for him and prized the opening out a bit to get at and sort the mess, but it's hardly ideal.

You won't be going up the mast in bad conditions and if you're not fit enough to get up aloft once you're in a calm place you too will be needing help. In mast furling also prohibits stiff sail battens.

Going up the mast is something you should be prepared to do, this isn't me but I've done it on both of my masts and on other boats to help other people out. You may need to replace a bulb in your navigation light, or replace an anemometer, or if you have in mast furling that's fouled up. Like this gentleman I used a climbing harness, but I subsequently changed it for a thing called a bosun's chair, far more comfortable if you're going to be up there a while. I rubbed down and re varnished my masts in this fashion, a long job! Alloy masts next time.

Another roller system is to have a roller running horizontally, just above the boom and roll the sail down instead of in. You don't see this so often and I've never used one. Again battens are likely to be a problem, but given you can get to the boom with your hands and any problems will be close to head height rather than way up aloft it seems an eminently sensible idea to me.

Unlike quite a few I've seen this catamaran does not have in mast furling, hurray, it does have a sail bag attached to the boom to catch the sail as you lower it, also hurray.

Rollers on the boom aren't all alike, I've seen a few different designs, but my own view is that I'd avoid in mast furling for the liveaboard travelling lifestyle especially if you anticipate solo periods or solo voyages. If the boat has slab, or a boom reefing system with lazy jacks or a bag I'd look on that favourably and ask questions of the vendor. Of course they'll say it's wonderful but you can always ask for a demonstration or a lesson in how it works if you're seriously interested in the boat and they want to sell it.

So far we've only talked about reefing the mainsail. Traditionally one didn't necessarily reef a Foresail so much as change it for a smaller one. These days, guess what, Foresails, even huge Genoas can be rolled up and since it's not rolling up into a tight slot or cavity it generally works. If it doesn't roll away as neatly as you'd like you can do it again when things calm down a little, but if it has rolled away in a sudden squall and it's not damaging itself or anything else then happy days.

This is my new, at the time, Genoa made in Turkey, which I was very impressed with, you can clearly see both blue sacrificial strips. When the sail was rolled away it was completely blue, with those strips protecting the white sailcloth from degradation by the sun when not in use.

You will notice that Jibs normally have a strip of blue canvas along the lower edge and the trailing edge. When the sail is rolled up correctly it should all look blue, not like a stripey Maypole. The blue canvas is called a sacrificial strip. It's there to protect the sail proper from the sun when it's furled. If it's not covering everything it can't do its job, either the sacrificial strip is too narrow or the sail isn't rolling up as it should. When the sacrificial strip has sacrificed itself sufficiently have a sailmaker replace it, a new sail will cost even more.

It's not necessarily the case, but it's probable tat the candy stripe effect on this roller furled foresail means that either the sacrificial strip is too small or that the sail hasn't rolled away quite as intended, in either of these scenarios sun damage is likely to occur to the white sailcloth sooner than it should.

On a modern boat the jib, usually a Genoa if it's a high performance modern Sloop slides up a groove in a roller that itself is integral with the forestay, that is the wire holding the mast up at the front, the ones at the sides are called shrouds, stays and shrouds constitute standing rigging as they hold masts up, ropes that hoist sails, or control them, or furl them are called running rigging. If a piece of running rigging breaks it's not usually disastrous, if standing rigging breaks and the mast goes overboard still partially attached you're in considerable difficulty.

This is why insurance companies want standing rigging renewed every ten years, although I personally think that's a bit draconian, but will generally leave you to act responsibly with your running rigging. So your foresail is mounted in a groove on a roller, a furling line will enable you to roll the foresail away completely or partially and as a rule they work well.

Older boats had the foresails hanked on to the forestay. That is there was a row of metal hooks that snap closed around the stay and the sail was raised or lowered using a halyard. With this system the sail slides up easily and virtually falls down when lowered, so you can quickly change a Genoa for a Staysail or a Staysail for a Storm Jib.

But so far we've only talked about Sloops we'll come on to other options in just a moment because there's one last feature I'd like to make mention of. That is the self tacking jib. Tacking is when you sail a zig zag course in order to progress against the wind. When you tack or go about it's quite easy to have the mainsail change side, it'll happen automatically, all you really have to do is control it so it doesn't slam across. Similar thing with gybing, but again this isn't a sailing course.

Most jibs or foresails need to be helped across as they have to clear stays and the mast; a big foresail overlapping the leading edge of the mainsail remember, comes quite a way back along the side of the boat. The solo sailor well out to sea will probably take very long tacks and not have to do this too often, but if you're restricted for space, between islands for example it can be a bit work intensive. Some yachts however, have self tacking jibs. There's normally a track on the foredeck with a slider for the sheets, the ropes that control the sail, to slide across from one side of the boat to the other. The jib has to be small enough to clear any obstacles, but again it's a system I approve of heartily for the solo sailor. My boat didn't have one but I did help a friend who'd been widowed to relocate her boat which did have one, oh so easy!

My own boat once again showing the cutter ketch rig, two foresails, a main and a mizzen, it's the two foresails distinguish it as a cutter and not just a ketch. It's possible to see the roller reefing devices at the bottom of the forestays, but you can also see that the sails are hanked on as they bow slightly between each hank.

So lets look at boats with two masts now, you'll not be needing three. The most common two masted boat is a Ketch which is what I had although technically it would be known as a Cutter Ketch because she could fly two foresails at once. By flying my Genoa and Staysail there's a slot created between the two and they work extremely well together if the wind isn't too strong for that amount of sail. The mast had two forestays, one from the top of the mast to the tip of the bowsprit for the larger Genoa and an inner forestay that attached lower down the mast and ran to the bow upon which was attached the smaller Jib or Staysail.

Both foresails had roller reefing but of a very early design whereby the sails were hanked on in the old traditional way and rolled up around the stay itself. Because the metal hooks were rolled up in there, I decided it was best to have each sail fully in or fully out so it wouldn't be pulled tight against the metal hooks. Nonetheless I loved my system, because I could have a small foresail, a big one, or two, which was quite enough flexibility. In an emergency I could quickly drop a sail as the hooks would fall down the stay once the halyard was released, rather than having to drag it down through a slot.

You're highly unlikely to find one like mine these days, but don't worry, modern foresails mounted on an open roller tend to roll away when you need them to and you can use that system to regulate the size of a sail because it won't be pulling against metal hooks if it's partially rolled up. It's a good design which is why it's near ubiquitous.

This is technically a Yawl, with the mizzen mast behind the steering position and the rudder.

The second type of two masted rig is called a yawl, the only difference is that the smaller mast at the back is mounted further back on a Yawl than a ketch, usually behind the steering with the boom of that mast extending backwards behind the boat. I've not sailed one, but it looks more awkward to me, more difficult to get your hands on things, in particular the boom and the Mizzen sail. The third type of two masted rig is a two masted Schooner, which has at least one square sail. I mention it because I did meet a couple doing the liveaboard thing on a lovely two masted Schooner and a beautiful thing she was, but it's very rare, I can't remember seeing one being advertised for sale of a suitable size so I'm leaving it there.

You can get a Sloop with two foresails and I've seen one with three, but your most likely options are a straightforward Sloop with two sails for your purposes or a Ketch, hopefully a Cutter Ketch. I say hopefully a Cutter Ketch because it's the rig I'd most want. With four sails I could always balance my boat and make it work without any real strain and I'd rather have the required sail area made up of four smaller sails in lighter conditions than two enormous ones because if things change, and they can change very suddenly, I can cope better with my smaller sails. Especially alone.

There's one more consideration. Just as we discussed the depth of the boat in relation to sailing up rivers and getting into places there are also overhead obstacles like bridges and overhead power cables. Lower masts are a similar advantage to a shallow draft. While I was at Seville a tall sloop came up river and as it passed under the power cables it got a nasty and very costly shock.

Personally I'll probably be looking for another Cutter Ketch, but a sloop with sensible reefing systems, which to my mind excludes in mast furling and a mast that isn't too tall, how tall is debatable, well it's something I'd consider if everything else called out to me as being right. Other opinions are available especially regarding in mast furling. Talk to your RYA instructor and surveyor, but remember not all sailors have lived aboard for years and sailed into hundreds of different harbours and anchorages. Something that's not too deep, not too tall and offers a flexible sail plan will suit you well.

Those with a little knowledge will observe that I haven't mentioned gaff rigged boats. A gaff is like a second boom on top of the mainsail. Instead of the mainsail narrowing to a point where it meets the mast, a gaff makes the mainsail much larger. It's also possible to fly a topsail above the mainsail. The more sail area you have flying the faster you'll drive the boat, until you've reached its hull speed, the terminal velocity the hull can physically achieve in other words, after that more sail just puts more and unnecessary load on the mast(s) and rigging.

Here's a rare thing, that horizontal spar on the forward mast, means she carries a square sail and marks her out as a Schooner, small enough to be a liveaboard for two people, this is a lovely yacht.

This is a classic gaff rigged racer with a top sail flying as well. Lovely to look at and fast, not the rig for me though. You can see how the gaff adds to the acreage of the mainsail but all that sail and a weighty gaff means more crew please.

You see gaffs on old sailing barges and classic racing yachts mostly, but it's not unheard of on a cruising yacht. One of my friends, a boat gypsy liveaboard, leading the lifestyle were discussing here, does live on a gaff rigged boat. I've ignored them till now because I wouldn't buy one myself. Great for the classic crowd who rarely if ever sail solo. A gaff adds quite a lot of weight to the sail as well as making it bigger so it's potentially hard work to raise and to control as you lower it, especially in an unexpected squall. I said earlier I don't like huge sails, which is why a I prefer a ketch, a gaff is just a way to make a large sail even larger and harder work for the solo sailor. In my opinion.

There are other rigs, very early in this book I mentioned a friend who'd converted a boat to a Chinese Junk Rig. She spoke very highly about how easy the boat was to sail solo and to reef. Another rig is the cat rig where the sail or sails have what looks like the frame attached to the sail of a windsurfer, again I've met the owner of a Freedom 35 who swears by that rig, but I've also seen a Freedom converted to a Junk Rig.

People have preferences and prejudices. I like the Freedom yachts which have free standing alloy or carbon fibre masts, I love the simplicity and not having to replace standing rigging, even though ten years is quite a long time. I'd give either Cat or Junk rig a chance, but I can't recommend or disavow on personal experience. If you're looking at something a little out of the ordinary, have a sea trial, see and feel how easy it is raise sails and lower them, to reef down with just one person doing the work and see how close you can get to the wind and what she feels like under different points of sail, then decide. I'd certainly give both of these alternative rigs a try. The battens in a Junk Rig aren't terribly heavy like a gaff but there are quite a few of them.

I have seen a catamaran with a Ketch rig, but as a general rule they tend to have one mast and a sloop style rig. So now you know!

CHAPTER 7
THE ENGINE AND MECHANICALS

The ability to motor in your sailing boat is crucial. If sufficiently skilled you might be able to sail into an anchorage, turn into wind in precisely the right spot drop the anchor at precisely the right moment, get it to hold and drop the sails and get a round of applause. In a crowded anchorage people will look at you aghast and wonder who you're going to hit first!

You can't sail into a marina full of expensive boats, least of all if it's your first visit, you'll need to motor in. If your motor or gearbox has failed you can sail close and then radio the marina and ask for assistance and they'll probably bring you in with a RIB and outboard. A RIB is a rigid inflatable boat, ie an inflatable dinghy with a fibreglass or plastic centre section.

You might want to motor because the wind has changed and you're just five miles from your destination where you can sleep soundly, but you won't make it in daylight now without motoring. It's always best to enter a marina, harbour or anchorage that's new to you, in daylight if you can. GPS is very accurate, usually to within ten metres but on very rare occurrences I've known it be up to a few hundred metres off. One of those times was entering a Greek anchorage in bad weather, so I wanted to get into the calm, at night. Fortunately, with the aid of hand held spotlights I was able to find the entrance, the GPS alone would have put me on the rocks.

I think it was noticeably off about three or four times in ten years, but on that occasion it could have been disastrous. I don't think it was a bad fix as it read the same the whole time I was there, I think the chart information in the machine was slightly off in each case, but what whatever the reason, do not have blind faith, at night, or in fog.

Motoring in fog makes sense as you make a noise others might hear and if you have it radar is a godsend. When sailing radar uses a lot of electrical power, motoring it's of no consequence. Radar will not pick up small rocks awash, but it will show you the shape of the land and if you compare it against the GPS Chart plotter you can find your way into a river mouth for example even in a thick fog. I've done it, just be aware that others may be doing it too and they may be much bigger than you. Use your fog horn, radar and eyes and ears and follow your training. If necessary, refer to the RYA literature supplied with your training. Thankfully fog is infrequent, so infrequent you may have forgotten the signals, so check the book and make sure your navigation lights are on.

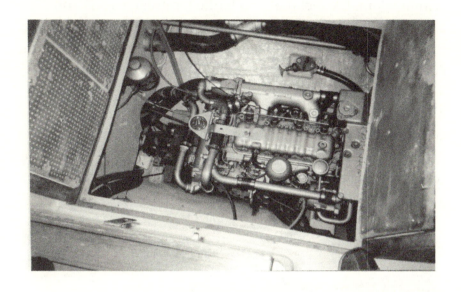

A good engine IS essential, this is an old Perkins, a well respected brand and despite its likely age look how clean and tidy everything is. This engine bay is a credit to the owner, take note, they won't all look like this. If they do it's a very good sign for you as a would be purchaser.

If you don't have radar you're probably safer staying well out to sea and keeping a good watch and waiting for the fog to clear. It's a strange thing but on land you hardly ever get wind and fog together, at sea that's not the case, so radar, although it's something you will rarely need is a marvellous thing when you do need it. AIS I didn't have. AIS identifies ships around you, it too would be a very good thing to have, it's on the checklist.

Commercial shipping tends to regard yachtsmen and women with disdain, the fact that you battle far greater odds and enter a far greater diversity of ports and so on means nothing to them, they are the professionals. If you need to ascertain the course of a commercial ship, and you may have several seemingly converging on you at once AIS will tell you. It will also help if you need to radio them. I've radioed ship in position such and such, having carefully worked it out and got no reply. If I've been able to use my binoculars and get the name and radioed using the ship's name they generally reply. The thing is you can't always make out the name.

Don't expect this big boy to get out of your way, he's probably restricted to a set channel anyway in a location like this, forget steam gives way to sail and stay away, if you need to start your engine so be it. Hence you need an engine that starts!

The old adage, steam gives way to sail really doesn't apply anymore. It's overruled in rivers and estuaries with dredged channels because the big ship is known as being constrained by draft, ie it can't turn because the channel it's in is the only place deep enough for it. Even at sea, might appears to be right, and don't assume professional sailors are keeping a good and responsible watch. It's rare and a criminal offence, but they've been known to hit and sink a yacht without even being aware they did it.

On one occasion I saw a cargo ship named 'Three Lochs' bearing down on me, I altered course but it seemed to alter course too, so I turned more abruptly and he too turned towards me once more, I started the engine and kept it in neutral, it could overpower the sails if necessary. Then I received a radio call from the Italian Captain of the cargo ship. In English it's the language of the sea thank goodness, we Brits being so appallingly lazy about learning the languages of others. The Captain just wanted to chat socially, he was intrigued by the design of my boat and thought her beautiful and wanted to know why I'd given her an Italian name! We had a very pleasant chat an although he came quite close I now knew he'd seen me and wouldn't hit me so no more changes of course were required, other than to get back on to my heading once he'd passed. It was a very pleasant incident I love the Italian attitude to life. It's never happened before or since, generally commercial traffic ignore you or see you as a nuisance I think.

Keeping the radio on is part of being 'on watch' at sea and I've heard some appalling racist conversations between officers on cargo ships of different nationalities one so bad I temporarily turned the radio off. Not all commercial shipping is what we'd truly think of as professional. Keep away from them as much as possible. You might turn out to be the more professional mariner in the end.

Avoiding several at once it might be much easier to start your engine, so it needs to be on the button, that is it needs to be a reliable starter when needed and your batteries and electrical systems need to be in good order.

Lastly, you might want to motor in order to avoid a storm. When I was in the Azores, the day I planned to leave, Tropical Storm Gordon was announced on the marina noticeboard as headed our way, the notice showed it's predicted path and likely time of arrival. The question now became wait it out in the marina, or try and get out of its path. The marina suffered a lot of swell, even in calm conditions the protection was dubious and boats were moving about and rubbing their fenders to death the whole time on the pontoons. The idea of being in that marina in a tropical storm appalled me. I've seen masts clash in a storm in a marina in Turkey. I decided to leave post haste and although my course to the Isles of Scilly should have taken me partly east as well as north I decided to use the calm before the storm to motor directly north and worry about east later. By going north in the calm before the storm I hoped the storm would pass below me as it tracked east north east.

Motoring in the calm before the storm was simply beautiful and we were accompanied for a few hours by a pod of very, very rare, North Atlantic Bottlenose Whales. Glorious. There are no garages at sea and not motoring club or automobile association vans packed with spare parts, tools and driven by a talented experienced engineer to come and rescue you. So don't wait for your instruments to tell you something is wrong, open the engine bay every hour while motoring, which in my case meant lifting a large section of the wheelhouse floor, and make a visual check.

I carried a good supply of tools, copious spanners and socket sets, mole grips, screwdrivers, scalpels, hammers, crowbar, hand brace (drill) and a wide range of types and kinds of drill bit. I had electric tools too, but they're not a great help at sea unless you have the battery kind and the batteries hold their charge well. I had saws and hacksaws large and small and spare blades, I also carried anything I thought might come in useful, nuts and bolts obviously, sailing spares like split links, shackles etc etc. and fortunately some rubber sheet. You never know when you might want to cover something with something that is an electrical insulator, batteries for example when you're working. I also had paper gasket material, instant gaskets, sealants, hose clips, and service items like oil and fuel filters, engine oil, all sorts, but you can't carry every spare part for your engine and gearbox.

On one of my visual checks I opened up the floor and to my horror saw engine oil all over the engine bay. I hadn't yet lost oil pressure, so no damage done to the actual engine which I immediately switched off. I had a Ford engine, a marinised tractor engine actually of about four litres, the Americans measure in inches not litres, producing 85HP. Wonderful thing, inherently reliable and this happened on my passage back to the UK so right at the end really, nor was the fault something inherent in the engine design.

My only gearbox failure had happened earlier that same year. Anyhow, my engine had a large steel block it holds a lot of heat and you can't work down there until it's cooled down, which even with the floor open and as much airflow as possible takes hours and hours and hours. So there I was wallowing around, no wind to sail with a tropical storm bearing down which had by this time, unbeknownst to me of course, become hurricane force, just waiting for hot metal to cool down so I could begin work.

You can't tell where an oil leak is when there's oil everywhere, so the first task was to make everything spotless so that I could top up the oil a little and start her to find the leak. Cleaning up took a several hours too. When I started her, fortunately I found the leak immediately and it was accessible which was a godsend, but I still had to fix it!

The leak was where the cable for the rev counter entered and the gasket had aged and failed. I disassembled it relatively easily but then had to manufacture a new gasket. My rubber sheet, cutting board and scalpels saved the day and I was able to manufacture a new strong, thick rubber gasket, which I then smeared with some instant gasket on both faces for a better seal and when I did everything back up good and tight with thread lock on the bolts it was instantly oil tight at the first time of asking and not about to vibrate loose.

I then filled the oil to the full level but the entire episode had taken about twenty four hours and cost, in calm seas, around one hundred and forty plus nautical miles, which is worth having under your belt with a storm coming! By the time I'd finished the wind was picking up so I sailed anyway! The wind direction allowed for a very broad reach, almost downwind in other words and knowing the storm was coming I was pretty soon on the Staysail only. Hurricane force winds hit me after dark and it was very dark with complete cloud cover and it was both terrifying and exciting in an adrenaline sort of way. My biggest worry was that I had a friend on board. If I'd killed myself then so be it, but I didn't want to be responsible for the death of another. However the story of the storm itself is for another book.

I hope I've convinced you that you need a reliable engine for convenience such as using canals and rivers where sailing is either impractical and or illegal and for entering marinas and harbours and anchorages, but most of all for safety, to get you home the last bit in daylight, to avoid shipping and just maybe avoid a storm.

Your gearbox and transmission or gearbox and propshaft are important too. I had a propshaft bearing failure once and the first engineer said the boat would have to be lifted out of the water, the rudder removed and the whole propshaft removed. A second, more resourceful engineer, or maybe one not looking to make more work and a bigger bill fixed it in situ and did a brilliant job. If you can get a second or third opinion do it and listen to the experiences of other sailors, liveaboard long enough something will fail.

I used to run a parachute club and have aircraft serviced, you'd think marine parts, given the need for safety at sea would be aircraft quality, sadly many are really not. Buy the best parts you can and keep everything properly greased and oiled as appropriate especially your stern gland, where the propshaft exits the hull into the water, a place where water might enter. There should be a bilge pump thereabouts and often a greaser you can refill and regularly turn a threaded plunger to force grease into the gland. The bearing that failed in my case was a sealed intermediate bearing, but eight years later when I sold the boat it was still absolutely fine.

This broken part in my gearbox in my last year of travelling caused me much heartache. It happened in Tunisia. With a great deal of help I recovered the other bit and a local fishing boat repair guy welded it for me, extremely well as far as the eye can tell. Nonetheless for safety's sake I waited to get a new replacement part from the USA which was quite an epic as things seemed to go astray in customs.

Gearboxes tend to be hydraulic or fully mechanical. I had a Paragon hydraulic gearbox it suffered one breakage in the last year, by which time it had given nearly forty years of service. The two types of gearboxes behave slightly differently. On my RYA course I was advised to put the gearbox in gear when sailing to prevent the prop spinning and make it less likely to wind up anything drifting past like old rope or fishing net. This was not possible with my hydraulic box, when sailing the water passing over the prop would turn it and that was that, I left her in neutral as a result. I don't think it caused me any problems and my prop was fitted with a rope cutter, it won't always work but I think it's worth having as there is so much junk in the seas.

When I was in a marina with the engine running the propeller would turn very slowly even in neutral, a bit of hydraulic pressure I suppose, but it meant, given the large propeller, that once cast off (untied) the boat would probably creep forward even in neutral unless there was sufficient headwind. You need to be aware of things like this especially if there is something in front of you. Take nothing for granted.

Treat your gearbox with respect, no gearbox and you may as well have no engine, other than for electrical charging and heating water, you won't be going anywhere under power without your gearbox. It only has three positions and usually a single lever that controls which gear you're in and as you move the lever further, forwards or backwards a second cable increases the engine revs, so the one lever is both gearchange and throttle. Usually but not always they're mounted fore and aft. Neutral will be in the middle, pull the lever back to engage reverse, move it further back to increase power. From neutral push the lever gently forwards to engage forward gear and gently push it further to gain more power.

You'll learn from experience what revs to use for maximum efficiency and range. Protect your gearbox by not slamming it from one gear to the other, before going into reverse drop the revs right down, then gently into neutral let the revs die completely and gently into reverse. Do similarly to go from reverse to forwards and allow time in your maneuvering to do this.

My gearbox failed in Tunisia. I found an engineer to help me, a fellow yachtsman actually and British so no language barrier, the selector that had broken was obvious and I ordered a new part from the USA. It never arrived, customs problem maybe. I ordered a second to be sent to a friend in the UK and she brought it out in her hand luggage. In the meantime, just in case I never got the new part, while my friend was still waiting I found a Tunisian workshop that could weld the old one back together.

I didn't want to trust to a weld so I hung on and the new part did ultimately arrive with my friend, the welded one went into the spare parts collection. I have to say though that the welded part looked superb. In poorer countries with a fishing fleet they're used to mend and make do and you'll find some very resourceful people as opposed to mere fitters. Never underestimate people, least of all because of an accident of birth.

So, we've established the importance of engine and gearbox, other mechanical items are important too, electrical or manual, such as winches for sailing and your anchor winch, for advice on this see my anchoring book.

Now you're probably waiting for me to recommend brands and I cannot really do that as I don't want to face litigation, although magazines write reviews all the time, I'm not a tester of new yachts, it's more about what type of thing is suitable for your objectives. In conversation with other sailors I have several times heard complaints about marine diesels from a particular Scandinavian car manufacturer. In particular that parts are no different from the car parts, just painted a different colour and overpriced. I cannot confirm or deny, but you have the choice of looking up the car part online if one is available and using that. Your decision.

I've heard good things about Buckh, Nanni and Yanmar dedicated marine diesels and to be honest I'd take almost any brand of normally aspirated diesel. I say normally aspirated, because I come back to that thing of their being no roadside rescue and recovery. I've had two turbocharged cars in my life and never a turbo problem so maybe I'm over cautious. My first turbo diesel car had over a hundred thousand miles on the clock when I sold it and the friend I sold it too did many more miles and was very happy with it.

Many mariners are I believe happy with their turbo diesels, but not all live on board permanently, cross oceans and place the same dependence on it that you will. You will find boats with all sorts of engines, often marinised car engines or a marinised tractor engine like mine. Ford and Mercedes engines are not uncommon, parts are available all over the world and they're pretty solid beasts, look after one and it should be reliable for donkey's years.

Some sailors swear by the old BMC diesel engines from London taxis. True, they have an incredible reputation in taxis for doing hundreds of thousands of miles of stop start driving. Personally I would try to avoid anything that is, or is becoming obsolete, so I'd tend to steer away. That and the fact that although the taxi engines had a good reputation BMC didn't always and the taxi community has plenty of mechanics and engineers who know that engine inside out other places around the world don't necessarily.

Back to the turbo debate and engines that are not turbo charged tend to be bigger and rev slower, they're inherently reliable and strong. Smaller engine, smaller parts, turbo pressure means more power from a smaller engine, my instincts alone tell me to steer away again. The turbo itself has moving parts that spin at speed, as I've said car turbos last very well in my experience but they're not living in damp salty air. Think on it. Do the RYA Diesel Engine Maintenance Course.

One of the things you will learn on your course is that diesel pumps and diesel injectors are machined to incredibly fine tolerances they are not something you'll mess with at all, least of all at sea. Your course will teach you the basics and about servicing but some things you just don't touch unless you're a fully qualified, experienced engineer with the right workshop equipment. There are already two things on that list, injectors and pump, a turbo makes it three.

I regularly and frequently used diesel fuel additives. My tanks were huge and I used the engine as little as possible because I like the calm of sailing and because my wallet likes the calm of sailing, as does my bank manager. Fuel preserver seems like a good idea when the fuel will sit for a long time. I also used copious quantities of injector cleaner in the fuel, not because I had clogged injectors, but to keep it that way, injector cleaner also keeps that vital pump clean too, win, win.

There are chemicals to deal with water build up in your diesel too. If you keep your fuel tanks nearly full there's not much of an air gap, but you can't keep them full the whole time so condensation is a risk. Your engine must have water separating filters, and any water that gets in, be it through condensation or contaminated fuel, should sink to the bottom, so the fuel take off should be very slightly higher than the bottom of the tank, but I'm a belt and braces kind of guy I used those chemical additives too.

The last one is an additive to deal with diesel bug. This is a subject in its own right! Nature is remarkably resourceful and as unbelievable as it sounds bugs can grow in diesel oil. Small microbes but enough of them and they can clog things up. I've heard it said that killing them with additives means they sink to the bottom and form a mass whereas if you leave well alone they'll pass safely through. I'm no expert but it seemed to me that bugs left to themselves would multiply and go on multiplying, so I used the additives frequently and I never had a problem. There you have my logic and my experience, you make your own decisions.

The final point about engines is cooling. A car has a radiator that is air cooled by the car moving forwards or by a fan if it's hot and stationary. A boat cannot use this system. Generally it has what's known as a heat exchanger, but some earlier boats used what is called raw water cooling. As with the majority of car engines the engine is cooled by water passing through cavities in the engine block. Raw water cooling simply pumps seawater or river water through the system. Lots of people have them, they work, they're simple, but you are pumping corrosive seawater through your engine and applying heat. Doesn't feel right to me.

The sea water is brought through a hole in the hull by a rubber impeller as a general rule. The impeller is like a rubber water wheel and the ends of the blades will be against the sides of the cavity they work in. Should the intake ever become blocked by a plastic bag, jellyfish or debris, then instantly there's no engine cooling, not only will the engine swiftly overheat and in the extreme seize up, but the impeller running dry will also self destroy very quickly indeed, so make sure you have plenty of spares and know how to fit them, have the vendor show you. The seas are dirty these days which is a great disgrace to mankind, but they are. Water that has passed through and done its job of cooling is ejected in spurts vis the exhaust. If you buy a boat with an impeller and most have them then regularly stick your head over and look at the exhaust to make sure it is spitting and keep an eye on your temperature gauge at other times.

A boat with a heat exchanger, most likely on modern boats still uses an impeller to bring in seawater which then cools the heat exchanger, which in turn cools the engine cooling water. Why do I and many others prefer this complication? It's because the engine cooling water is now a closed system, pipes carrying it run through the heat exchanger but the engine itself is cooled with nice, less corrosive fresh water, to which anti freeze and corrosion inhibitors are added. Just like your car. You still have to keep an eye on your temperatures and keep spare impellers and watch your exhaust, but I think it's a better system.

This is Francesca out of the water after another few years, for antifouling, anodes where necessary and cleaning of things like sonar heads, water speed log, propeller and so on, but that big pipe running along the top of the keel is a section of the keel cooling system. I'm sure it created some drag, but from a maintenance and reliability point of view, the envy of many of my fellow sailors.

The option you're least likely to find is keel cooling, it's so rare that on occasion in marinas concerned sailors would come running up to me shouting a warning 'there's no water coming out of your exhaust!'. In fact I had what's known as Keel Cooling. My engine had fresh water cooling, with a header tank like a car and antifreeze and corrosion inhibitors, but instead of the pipe running through a heat exchanger, where seawater is pumped in to cool it, the water pipe simply went outside the boat to the sea! It ran along one side of the keel, then back along the other side and back in through the hull. Being a steel boat the piping for this purpose was large bore steel piping, welded in place, watertight and strong as you like.

It's probably less practical on a fibreglass or wooden boat, but even steel boats don't have it that often. The advantages are obvious, no blocked intake ever, no impeller change, precautionary or otherwise, ever. Completely sealed, in the ten years I used it, bulletproof. Drawbacks are it causes a bit of drag for sure and my boat was never going to be fast. Keep the boat stationary for a long time with the engine running, for example waiting for a lock or bridge to open and the keel pipes will actually heat the stationary water around them or maybe with the revs at tick over the pump didn't manage that great length of pipe so well, but it would eventually start to get hot if the boat wasn't moving. Small prices to pay and a great system, but don't expect to find it. If you do it's a bonus, if you buy a steel boat that doesn't have it you may be able to convert. However, the vast majority of people live happily with a heat exchanger and a supply if impellers. You just really don't want the impeller to fail or clog at a crucial time.

I've not heard about gearbox failures from other sailors so I'm working on the basis that they generally cut the mustard. Change the oil periodically, keep a visual check for leaks, neither engines nor gearboxes run long without lubrication and follow the service schedules for engine and gearbox. Read the manual, for hydraulic boxes you might need to check the level when it's hot.

So, once again we've discussed the features and options; you'll need to make your own decisions as a sailor, but the major things to weigh up, I believe I've covered for you. Once again talk to people. Often your surveyor won't run the engine. Out of the water this can be difficult as you'll need to plumb in cooling water as a rule and so the engine often isn't part of the survey, much as I'd like it to be. If that's the case get a sea trial, look for smoke, listen to it, if it has an impeller, as is likely, make sure water is coming from the exhaust, make sure it revs as it should, check oil pressure and temperatures, look for leaks and that's pretty much the best you can do. If there are receipts that's a good sign but many of us do our own oil changes and so on.

My own boat had a built in wobble pump to pump out old engine oil, what a godsend, ask how the vendor does oil changes. Many people have to put a thin plastic tube down the dipstick pipe with a hand pump, usually brass and resembling a bicycle pump on top to extract old engine oil which needs to be hot to be thin. It's messy, time consuming, hot and difficult. Your engine will be mounted low in the boat, you cannot get under it to drain the oil as a rule, so ask how it's done. Now we can look at the features and onboard equipment you as a liveaboard, will need, find desirable or can live without.

CHAPTER 8
WHAT FEATURES ARE ESSENTIAL, DESIRABLE, UNNECESSARY

If you take a survival course you'll be taught that the first essential is shelter, after that come food and water, but you'll die sooner without water than you will without food. Your boat already provides you with shelter from the elements, although once again I have to say my wheelhouse was a joy and I can't imagine buying a boat with an open cockpit now.

So, water tanks are of course essential, I had two very large tanks and I could have one turned off, isolated from the other in case of contamination or leakage. I think this is a fine idea. Being careful about how much I used for showering I could make my water last three months. My boat was also equipped with a watermaker. A watermaker draws water from the sea, forces it through a membrane at more or less the molecular level, a bit like osmosis and turns sea water into drinkable water.

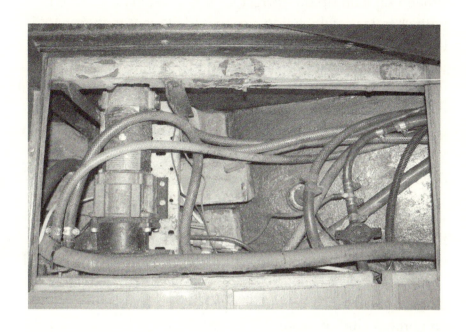

This is my never used watermaker. The bricks are actually lead ingots used for ballast and that's not rust it's bronze coloured paint, there was some rust there previously I have to admit. A couple of the hose clips left by my predecessor aren't stainless, they should be, something to look for.

You don't want to be using it in polluted water or where debris and flotsam are likely to get in and block things up, but in mid ocean it could be a very good thing. The point about a watermaker is it needs to be used or laid up, not simply left and used every couple of months because things will start to grow in it and the water it produces might then make you ill which pretty much negates the point of it.

When I say laid up the correct term is 'pickled', it's treated with chemicals, which you also wouldn't want to ingest, to keep things from growing in it. The manual will tell you how to do this and what you need to do to reinstate it. A watermaker for a yacht is likely to be electric, there are manual watermakers but they're hard work. Due to the pressure required the watermaker will need a lot of electrical energy so you'll only want to use it with the engine, or if you have one a generator running.

When I purchased my boat, the watermaker was pickled. I flicked the switch momentarily to see if the motor ran and never, ever touched it again for the duration of my ten years. If I took a long voyage I also took a few plastic containers of extra fresh water so I could enjoy showers, but again I'm a belt and braces kind of bloke.

As well as being able to alternate tanks and isolate one I used water purification chemicals and tablets available for camping, sailing etc from outdoor suppliers, you can buy them in bulk online. Try to ascertain they won't interfere with, or corrode whichever material your fresh water tanks are made of and stick to the dosage recommended, you'll be drinking the stuff.

Imagine you're at sea and all your electrics fail, that's a problem in itself but if the tap no longer works because the electric pump has no power you'll feel the loss of drinking water, more than the loss of even your navigation aids. Make sure there's a foot pump, mine was under the sink, with a separate pipe leading over the sink. Having drinking water and not being able to access it is the stuff of madness, followed by mortality.

So one water tank is obviously essential, two better, a watermaker proved to be unnecessary in my scenario where I had two water tanks and kept them healthy. Food is the next essential. Boats come with lockers, lockers everywhere, under seats, under beds, in the wheelhouse or cockpit, in the galley (kitchen). Fill them with clothes and gear by all means but leave enough space to enable you to provision for a long voyage. There's lots of advice I could give about marking tins with permanent markers in case labels disintegrate and so on but this is about what type of boat to buy.

Some have freezers, again a big electrical drain, mine had a relatively small fridge, top loading, not the easiest for finding things, but no door to fly open in a rough sea. It had one cold plate on one of the four sides, it was roughly square, the lid when in place was part of the galley work surface.

So far we've been pretty much talking about survival, merely existing, but you didn't choose this lifestyle to merely exist. I'll proffer the opinion that although you can carry food without one and fresh fruit and vegetables can be hung up in nets, a fridge that you can run all the time is essential.

In a marina you can plug into shore power, so running the fridge, no problem, in some fishing harbours power might not be available to you and in anchorages it absolutely won't be. So, if the fridge is essential, so is adequate electrical power. My boat had two truck starter batteries, to turn over the four litre, Ford diesel and four deep discharge domestic batteries. I also had two solar panels on the wheelhouse roof and a powerful wind generator.

Batteries designed to start cars, vans, trucks and tractors are designed to give a lot of power in short bursts. The engine starts and recharges them, they last a lot better if kept fully charged. Deep discharge batteries are designed to give a smaller amount of power over a longer period and to be able to discharge almost completely and still recover when charged. You do not want to be using starter batteries for domestic purposes, your boat must have both.

My domestic batteries were of a type used for powering golf carts. They were lead acid like the starter batteries but with very different plates. The brand was Trojan. They are six volt but were mounted in pairs to give a twelve volt supply. I found them very very long lasting and excellent in all regards, except that they did need topping up with distilled water pretty frequently in hot climates. They were mounted on a rack in the engine bay not far below the deck, making access to them a real game. I believe there are systems which allow you to top up one water container which will feed the individual cells of multiple batteries as they require it. I've been told about this by another yachtsman but never seen one. It sounds like an excellent idea.

The sailor who was a qualified electrician and who fixed an electrical problem that baffled me, commended me for having Trojans, he said he'd swapped his for gel batteries, theoretically sealed for life, no servicing etc, but he'd had no end of problems and wanted his Trojans back. I believe they're manufactured in the USA, but I've seen them for sale in Turkey so I think they're widely available, certainly in the UK. There must be other golf cart batteries too.

Having a bulletproof electrical system is vital to your peace of mind, standard of living and safety. If you need the engine to start it must start. You should have a four way switch that allows you to select, starting batteries, or domestic, or both, or have everything off so you can work on things safely.

In an emergency you can then use your domestic batteries to give a little help to the starting batteries. Most importantly never forget to have the starting batteries isolated while sailing, the domestic batteries should be able to run your chart plotter and radio and when you're close to shore your depth sounder and if necessary your radar, as well as your fridge and water pumps. That said, engine on for radar, it enables swift avoiding action as well as making sure of the electrical supply.

Your engine should have a powerful alternator, some yachts, bigger ones generally, have a diesel generator in the engine bay as well as the engine. I wouldn't be looking for that specifically when shopping for a boat. You can get a small petrol generator, some are the size of a large suitcase, in fact I believe they're called suitcase generators.

If you forget to isolate your engine starting batteries after starting, then switch off the engine and sail and start using the starting batteries for navigation etc at sea unaware you're doing so, then having a way to quickly charge them up could be a lifesaver, but I don't think it's essential to have a second diesel engine effectively just for that purpose. Petrol, or gasoline if you're reading this in America, is explosive and dangerous, but you'll carry a small amount for your outboard or outboards anyway and a small petrol generator isn't terribly thirsty. Of course a full on diesel generator is much like being plugged into the mains, but it will make noise and be another expense and not especially good for the environment if you use it a lot.

My boat had one deficiency, electrically speaking, and that was a good control panel showing the condition and charge in the batteries. I tied up the wind generator, so it couldn't spin whenever I ran the engine to try and avoid overcharging, I checked my batteries frequently for electrolyte level and put a hand meter on them, but I should have got around to a proper control panel and a regulator. There was actually a regulator fitted, but I never entirely trusted it.

On sunny, windy days I had no worry about a shortage of electrical power for fridge, radio, navigation etc, but at night, in light winds insufficient to turn the wind generator there would be a drain on the system when sailing. Also at anchor, since you need to run an anchor light to avoid people running into you, that's another legal requirement too. On nights when it gets dark early you may well want interior lighting as well and maybe music.

One way to protect your batteries is to drain them as little as possible. Quartz halogen bulbs use significant amounts of power, led bulbs hardly any, a worthwhile change. I also carried old fashioned oil lamps, they don't provide a lot of light, but better than nothing if the electrics fail and they produce heat which is great in winter, not so great if it's a hot night, options though.

You can have a powerful wind generator that produces a worthwhile amount of juice but which needs a decent breeze to turn it, and therefore produces nothing at all much of the time, especially in sheltered anchorages, or a very light one that hardly ever stops turning no matter what, but which isn't generating a lot.

I've seen yachts with both and catamarans with one of each type, one on each hull. You pays your money and takes your choice but I'd have a couple of fair sized solar panels and at least one wind generator minimum. If the boat you're looking at doesn't have them, you will need to add them and the requisite wiring and regulators etc if you're going to be a gypsy and go where you will. In fact there's a catamaran pictured earlier in the book with two wind generators although both of the same type.

So, we have a fridge to keep our food fresh and an electrical system that's bulletproof to run it. What about cooking food and probably more important, making comforting hot drinks. You won't be cooking electric unless you're plugged into shore power and you won't want to cart two cookers around, space is at a premium, so bottled gas it is. Usually Calor, could be propane. Calor gas freezes at very low temperatures and can be found in southern Sweden, but rarely, and further north forget it.

I used Calor, went to Sweden and Norway in summer only and made sure I had about five tanks of the stuff before leaving. However I did have a propane regulator on board as well, left by the previous owner. The Calor gas bottles can be exchanged or refilled in many places, the cost varies by country but I never found it too scary. Anyhow you need it. Carry a propane regulator and make sure your cooker grill and rings can work with it by all means. In some parts of the world it might be all you can get.

The big issue with gas is it's jolly dangerous, it can explode. A yacht suffered a gas explosion in a marina while I was there. One person on board was blown up through the deck and killed instantly, the other had life changing injuries. If gas leaks it sinks downwards, it's heavier than air, it can build up in the bilges, silent and deadly until you light something or even just use an electrical switch.

The gas bottles should be in a dedicated locker with a drain to the outside world. In addition you should have gas detectors in the bilges and gas locker, and I carried a couple of hand held ones so I could prod around from time to time, belt and braces! The gas bottles could be secured on deck, but then they'd be open to rain and salt spray, any decent boat will have a proper gas locker and drain.

However, the gas has to come inside to reach the cooker and hob, so make sure the pipes are approved for the purpose and that they're in good condition. Pipes might be metal or rubber or you might have a bit of both. Rubber pipe should be replaced by a qualified gas engineer every few years. Quiz the vendor about the gas system.

When you use gas, use it and water sparingly, if you're making two mugs of tea use the mugs to measure the water into the kettle so as to waste nothing, gas and water will last longer and there will be fewer spillages. Fill mugs no higher than three quarters full when sailing in any kind of waves and have mug holders scattered around the boat plus non slip mats. Just saying.

Now you have shelter, water, food and you can cook. If you eat and drink something is going to come out the other end from time to time. The heads are essential, there will be at least one loo on any boat that's going to be a liveaboard. Traditionally they have a hand pump that brings in seawater with one stroke, you don't want to be using precious sweet water to flush the toilet, and sends it all out again with the next stroke. Electric toilets are now available, which for gypsies like us are probably a bit over the top and another level of complication and drain on the batteries I'd leave them to the gin palaces.

I'm told that most yachtsmen who wash up on beaches have their flies open. Well, I'm guilty of taking a leak over the side, but do it on the lee side for hopefully obvious reasons and be very, very careful. If anyone from the RYA is reading this NEVER do it at all and never go on deck without clipping on and wearing a life jacket!

Having a toilet is essential of course and these days you need more than that, you need a holding tank. A holding tank for black water, that is toilet water, is a legal necessity in some countries and in Turkey now they expect you to have a holding tank for grey water, that is water you've washed in, or done the washing up in too. You could collect it in a bowl and direct it to the black water tank via the toilet, but it would be difficult to prove if you were challenged.

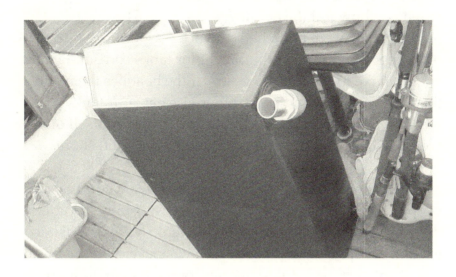

This is a new, larger black water holding tank I had custom made for Yacht Francesca in Turkey.

My boat came with a black water tank. There was a filter in the heads to deal with fumes and I could remove that and use the pipe for pump out purposes through the porthole. Bit of a bugger really. Clearly old boats were not designed with modern regulations in mind. In Turkey I had the holding tank changed for a much larger one after, with two people on board, we managed to fill the existing one. I can't remember the litres now but when comparing boats compare the size of holding tank or tanks. Make sure there is a robust valve to switch from out to sea and into holding tank, it's one of the things I had to change.

I did come across an expensive Oyster yacht that had gauges to tell you how full the holding tanks were. The owner reported they were not reliable, which was ironic as he'd made his money making such equipment for tanks containing milk and suchlike for the food industry. If the boat has them and they work, all well and good, otherwise get your tanks pumped out as frequently as you can, or do it yourself outside the legal limit. Which is generally twelve miles off shore.

I've seen boats discharging holding tanks in anchorages where people are swimming from the beach. Disgusting and utterly defeats the point of having a holding tank. It's always felt to me that pumping straight out to sea whenever you use the loo is probably less harmful to the environment than dumping a big tank load all at once, but if you can get it pumped out in a marina and they deal with it responsibly and don't just put it straight through a pipe into the sea then that's the best thing. When I was far from land I just pumped to sea when I used the loo. When I was in a marina I used their toilets and showers. In anchorages, or close to shore and people I used the holding tank.

Now, we've just mentioned showers. A built in shower, if you're in a hot climate is not actually essential, unless discharging grey water is illegal. I quite often used a shower bag hung in the rigging and showered on deck. They're sold for camping, black on one side to heat the water from the sun. Be careful they can get very hot if left too long. If there are other boats around you can always shower in your swimwear, although some nationalities seem not to worry and of course you can take a swim and just use sweet water to rinse the salt off.

The beauty of a shower bag is that it forces you to consider and ration the water. All that being said, you won't always be in hot places, winter comes and a power shower is the kind of luxury that makes the difference between existing and enjoying the lifestyle. The power comes from the electric pump that also supplies the tap. The hot water is worth looking into when you buy the boat. My own had a hot water tank just in front of the heads, accessed from the forward sleeping area. It had a calorifier or immersion heater, that worked from shore power, or you could use it with a generator if your generator is powerful enough. The other way to get hot water would be to run the engine for half an hour.

A switch in the wheelhouse turned on a pump under the main cabin sole that pumped water along a pipe that led through into the engine bay, through the header tank of the engine, but not mixing with it of course and back to the hot water tank. Whenever I needed the engine I made hot water, the tank was well insulated and it stayed hot for many hours. Both shower and sink had mixer taps. Bliss.

My hot water tank under the forward bunk could be heated electrically by shore power or by a pump that ran water along a pipe through the header tank to make use of heat generated when the engine was running. Didn't take long to make a full tank either. In hot climates I used a shower bag in the rigging, in the UK or the Baltic hot water is a blessing.

Most yachts of thirty feet plus will have a hot water system of some kind. Ideally you want both hot water from shore power and hot water from your engine. If you're going to run an engine and generate heat use it!

Hardy folk may not worry about heating or air conditioning, but you wouldn't buy a house without heating and in a hot climate you would at least consider air conditioning. Most of the boat gypsies that I met did not have air conditioning, but a few had the portable kind. Really large yachts often have it built in. In many marinas, less so in the UK, but in quite a few abroad electricity and water are not metered and are included in your fees.

I carried a couple of small fan heaters that could also blow air without heating it, but to keep cool I relied more on a fabric chute designed to catch the wind like a small spinnaker sail and direct it down through the largest hatch. Other sailors I met had large fans that turn this way and that on a stand, the sort of thing you find in an office and too big for a small boat in my own view. Whether you catch the wind, or use fans, or a portable aircon unit the choice is yours, space is limited, but the power to run such a toy might be effectively free! Steel boats in particular can get very hot inside in summer and cold in winter. Insulation is essential as has previously been mentioned in relation to condensation and rust.

A boat is a small space to heat, but heating is desirable, even in the Mediterranean it can get cold in winter and like me you may want to venture further afield. I found one fan heater sufficient in winter, in a marina with inclusive electricity, the second one was as you've rightly surmised, a backup.

My boat actually came with heating plumbed in. It's like a mini diesel furnace in the engine bay, with large air ducts running to outlets in each cabin and the heads. Central heating! The thing was very effective and because it used diesel from the main tanks, no extra or different fuel needed to be carried. The main brand is Eberspacher. Mine was of the type that used to be used to heat trains, it was really too big for the boat although it certainly did the job and could be used at sea with the engine running.

It was very susceptible to voltage drops and might not always fire up as a result, there was a small filter that frequently needed cleaning or changing and even though I carried spare parts for it I rarely used it because of the overkill and potential hassle. If the boat you're looking at has one fitted, if it's up to date, ie newer than mine and properly serviced, and if it's a sensible size for the boat you'll probably love it.

The main alternative is a thing called a Taylors Stove, other brands may well be available, but this is a diesel stove that looks a bit like a small solid fuel stove. It has a chimney that will protrude on deck and needs, obviously, to be protected from water ingress at sea. I'm told they're very economical and simple and those two things appeal greatly to me. I haven't tried one, but I'd happily buy a boat which had one, or which had an appropriately sized and well maintained modern Eberspacher or Webasto heating, similar system. These systems would be expensive to buy and install, not impossible by any means, but I'd mark up a boat with appropriate levels of heating.

A diesel stove like this is simple, economical and effective, but only in the one cabin. If you want heating ducted throughout the boat look for an Eberspacher or Webasto system.

I have come across liveaboards with solid fuel stoves, but as an international traveller you won't be wanting to cart the fuel, so steer clear.

Living and not merely existing means you want music at least and maybe other forms of entertainment such as TV, DVD player, computer, internet. Some liveaboard type boats have these built in. Especially now we have flat and smart TVs. It's not essential if you can use portable equipment. My own boat had a Radio CD player like you found in cars until recently and a TV with video player mounted on a high shelf in the main cabin. I took the latter down as being too heavy and dangerous in my view. I played music a lot, and didn't miss the TV. In fact at sea I even rejected the idea of a satellite phone as I thought I really wanted to be alone with the elements. Of course there's a safety advantage to a Sat Phone and they've come down in price. Ex rentals are very affordable, your call but you're unlikely to get one with the boat.

WiFi is available in most marinas, a computer isn't likely to come with the boat but carrying a laptop and smartphone is done by everyone these days, except maybe one or two even more eccentric than me.

Having mentioned safety now as well as creature comforts certain things are essential. A VHF radio for communication with an aerial at mast head for maximum range. Range varies with weather conditions but thirty miles is usually max and it could be a heck of a lot less. It is needed to talk to shipping that's close by and to port officers and marina staff when you get close. Essential and have at least one hand held as back up, or to use from an outside steering position if yours is in the wheelhouse or cabin. Solo you can't be in two places at once. As mentioned previously it's a legal requirement, although I don't know if it would be enforced somehow, but it's common sense to have it and to have it on.

For longer range, very, very long range you could have a single sideband radio as used by radio hams. Could be very useful for picking up weather information and getting messages home and SOS, but largely superseded by Sat Phones these days. I have one but never got around to fitting it or really felt the need. Installation is a big job with lots of copper insulation. Compared with a Sat Phone it is free to use once installed but there will be fewer people listening these days.

Weather information is vital and there's a system called Navtex which is a little receiver with a screen that gives weather and hazard warnings as text in English and updates periodically if you're within range of a transmitter, which you generally are if you're coasting. There's a big difference between coasting reasonably close to shore and crossing oceans. Near the coast you can use your cell phone very often and if you have a data plan you can probably even get on line for weather information from a host of met office and specialists such as Wind Guru.

I didn't use a mobile phone much at all on account of budget. I got weather forecasts via marina WiFi when using marinas and in anchorages I used Navtex, or spoke with richer yachtties anchored nearby. You can very often do that by VHF radio, you don't need to get into your dinghy and go knocking necessarily.

Get several forecasts and you'll probably get conflicting information, but you'll find a service you trust on the whole or you can go with the majority opinion. Anyhow, make sure and ask how the vendor gets weather information.

AIS we've touched on already it's not essential but the simple read only version would be very attractive to me, a boat that had it would score points over one that didn't and radar the same. Automatic electric bilge pumps are a must, call me old fashioned but I believe water should be outside the boat. Powerful manual bilge pumps are also a must in case of electrical failure and guess who also carried a couple of hand held ones with pipes that could get in just about anywhere.

The checklist at the back of this book lists safety equipment, such as liferaft, lifejackets, Danbuoy, horseshoe life rings, flares use it. And have a grab bag of essentials to go into a liferaft with you, but I say again I'm not trying to teach you everything you need to know, just to buy the right boat with appropriate equipment. More information on safety equipment will be found in Chapter 12.

I haven't mentioned clothes washing which is essential, but it's something I did by hand in a large, cheap, strong black rubber bucket, that got hot in the sun. I dried clothes and bedding in the rigging. Some marinas don't like it, makes the place look untidy. I'm a rebel, do it unless told to stop. Some liveaboard boats have washing machines and I have seen one you turn by hand rather than use electricity, but I see a washing machine as quite a luxury. If a boat doesn't have one I won't score it down, if does have one I probably wouldn't score it up either. The space might be more useful. Of course if you're a non travelling kind of liveaboard, different matter, you can have pot plants and all sorts a gypsy won't carry.

My boat had a removable table for the wheelhouse, put it up in port, take it down to travel. I carried a travel iron and if I really wanted to be smart I'd iron something on a towel spread over the table. Rarely wanted to be that smart!

Since I hoped my daughter would visit I also carried some toys, softball, frisbee, volleyball for the beach, American football and soccer ball and an inflatable kayak, all very optional. Oh and folding bicycles times two!

I'm sure I've forgotten something but I hope I've focussed your mind on what's essential, desirable or what's a bit more than is really needed or warranted. The checklist at the back should really help. That's the idea anyway!

One of my folding bicycles in Sweden.

CHAPTER 9
HOW SHOULD I GO ABOUT FINDING MY BOAT

When I was looking for my first large boat the traditional place to look was yachting, sailing and boating magazines from Yachting World to Practical Boat Owner. There are still magazines and some have an online presence as well. There are other titles in other countries and in other languages if you're a linguist, but it shouldn't be necessary.

Some magazines no longer carry so much advertising now we have the internet, so go to a newsagent and look. I found the boat I eventually bought in an advertisement placed by a yacht broker, Williams And Smithells. There are certain advantages to using a broker. It is usual to make an offer subject to survey, having paid the deposit to the broker it is then incumbent on them to return it should the surveyor come up with too many problems.

What constitutes too many problems is open to debate and interpretation however and the broker won't want to lose the sale, nonetheless their reputation is also important to them. The thing is that you've paid for the survey, you won't get the money back for that, clearly you were a serious genuine buyer, if you don't like what the surveyor has said you must be able to walk away.

Naturally all boats have something a surveyor won't like so it's possible to haggle and you don't want to walk away over something trivial. In my case the first boat I wanted clearly had too much work to do. At least in the surveyor's opinion if not in the vendor's. Nonetheless the deposit was returned and that wasn't via a broker, the majority of yachtsmen and women strike me as pretty decent sorts.

If you don't know about brokers then a broker is a company or individual paid to sell a boat on behalf of the owner; it works in a similar way to an estate agent. A good broker will take care of a lot of the background work to make the sale easier for both the parties. Although the vendor will pay commission to the yacht broker, there's no charge to the buyer officially, the broker's commission may well be reflected in the price of the boat.

What are the possible benefits of buying a boat via a broker? When a boat is being sold through a brokerage company, the broker should be able to answer any questions you have about it. The broker should be familiar with the vessel and be able to tell you about the condition of the boat, or give you more information to help you to understand if it's the right boat for you. If the brokerage is in the marina where the boat is based or if it's a few miles up the road that should hold true, but I have seen boats all over the world on a single broker's list, I have my doubts that any broker is intimately acquainted with them all.

The internet will allow you to view pictures and descriptions in English, of boats in many different countries. Brokers likewise have boats scattered far afield very often. Some brokers are franchises and or have branches in many countries. I came across several called Boatshed whilst travelling.

If the boat isn't for you, a yacht broker might well have other boats on their books that you may want to consider.

A yacht broker is generally going to be up to speed on all the paperwork involved with buying a boat. They will organise the documentation outlining your offer, formalise the terms of sale, compile an inventory and check the VAT documentation, ease transfer of title and can advise about Small Ships or full registration. This eases the administrative burden on you as the buyer.

When it comes to a sea trial, some brokers will sometimes attend with you. They should be able to help you if you're not sure how everything works on board and answer any questions about running and maintenance costs, although the vendor probably knows more about those things and the broker is being paid by him so is likely to agree with whatever you're told.

My broker didn't attend the viewing in Ireland and as I've said it's unlikely they will if there's a big distance involved however, the broker did provide a good level of service once the sale had completed especially with regard to insurance.

A broker may be able to help you find a mooring, refer you to boat clubs and point you in the direction of the best place to get your boat maintained, but I did my own research in that regard and I'd suggest you do the same. Boat shows often bring a number of marinas to exhibit pictures of their facilities, discuss prices, deals and if a chain of marinas how a berth holder in one of the firm's marinas can visit others at no or lower cost.

Boat shows and boat jumbles also helped me equip myself and since the marketplace for lines, fenders, lifejackets, gps AND marinas is competitive at such events you can save more than the cost of entry. Southampton Boat Show has eclipsed London and Beaulieu Boat Jumble is about the biggest of those events. Brokers may also exhibit at boat shows, there are even likely to be used boats for sale at such events these days as well as new.

Make sure you use an established, reputable broker if you're going to use a broker. A broker going bust just after taking your deposit would be a nightmare.

The second boat I surveyed, not through a broker, would have been fine with £6000 worth of remedial work to the hull but it was at the top of my price range, so I needed the vendor to drop the £6,000 off the price, he offered to split it with me but even that was too much for me as I wanted to keep money back for other improvements and travelling. Besides which it was his boat had a crack in it, which the survey I'd paid for revealed to his benefit! Again the deposit was returned by the vendor, again a fair guy.

The third boat I had surveyed needed quite a lot doing but was sound in all the key departments so I decided to go ahead, I think you have to be reasonable. As mentioned earlier, no sooner had I bought boat number three than the owner of boat number two came back and said he'd drop the price by the required £6,000.

That was too late, serious buyers are often in short supply, lots of dreamers and what a car dealer would call tyre kickers. The fact that you are serious gives you a lot of clout. If you're willing to pay a deposit and pay for a survey you're clearly serious. Play that card.

These days there are many ways to find boats, usually online, there are a few online platforms and websites such as apolloduck and ybw. You can simply google the type of boat you're looking for and you'll soon find other sites too. For example if this is what you've decided try steel ketch for sale, Westerly yacht for sale, Colvic Watson yacht for sale, Halberg Rassey yacht for sale. Even without 'for sale' in the search term you'll probably find something try just Freedom 35, Morgan 41, Oyster Yacht, Moody Yacht, Van Der Stadt, Island Packet, Formosa Yachts, Beneteau, Jenneau, Nicholson, Sweden Yachts and so on if you know the names of types you're interested in.

If you want something small to start out and give things a try, search MacGregor or trailer sailer, trailer sailor, Beneteau First.

The more advertisements you look at the more you'll get an idea of what the different types are like, try Finnsailer, Nauticat, LM, MacWester, Amel, Barbican or just try Liveaboard, Motor Sailer, Motor Sailor, Passage Maker, Wheelhouse Ketch, or 35ft sloop if that's what appeals to you.

Of course you can try catamaran for sale, aluminium yacht, bilge keel yacht, drop keel and lifting keel yacht, steel yacht, you could try searching for a Spray; inspired by Captain Joshua Slocumb and his book Sailing Alone Around The World, which I'd highly recommend, a few replicas of his boat The Spray have been built, with varying degrees of accuracy and usually in steel, could be a great liveaboard and I know a lady who has one, who has travelled widely and survived all manner of bad weather.... Anyhow I'm sure you can think of plenty of other search terms too.

Don't forget to search for UK Marinas and UK Yacht Brokers, substitute UK with USA, Canada, France, Spain, Italy, Mediterranean, Caribbean, Azores, Canaries, European as necessary.

The odd one out in in terms of online sales platforms, in a way is Ebay that well known online auction site. I'd certainly keep an eye on that, the market is really down at the time of writing but even so I saw a Freedom 35 in very good condition sell for £13,000 roughly at auction. Not so long ago it would have been £30,000 and could be worth that actually, I almost wished I'd placed a bid.

Some sailors who are retiring from sailing will auction their boats with a low reserve. Occasionally a boat is auctioned with no reserve. Someone who has inherited a boat, doesn't know a lot about the boat and who doesn't want to be lumbered with berthing fees, insurance, and maintenance might well find Ebay attractive, just move it on.

Other vendors who love their boat might over value it and hold out losing money as a result. Occasionally a marina takes ownership of a boat where the owner has defaulted for a long time on their berthing fees, that boat is often auctioned. HM Customs or UK Police will impound a boat used for drug smuggling or other illegal purposes and that may end up at auction*, not necessarily Ebay. However, bargains are out there so do your research. As indeed you've started to do!

I think it's true to say that Ebay attracts motivated sellers, so if you're a motivated buyer it could be a good match. If the boat is auctioned and you place the highest bid you're obliged to buy it. I'm not sure how well it's policed by Ebay, or whether anyone would bother taking legal action. Not likely is my conclusion, since I auctioned my boat on Ebay, the purchaser presumably changed his mind as he denied bidding and said he must have been hacked! Fortunately I found another buyer later. You can report people who mess you around and if you're the seller you have to let Ebay know that the buyer didn't pay or they'll possibly charge you the commission!

For these purposes of course we're talking about buying. I know the Freedom 35 that sold for £13,000 was a good one because my neighbour, also an experienced sailor, went to look at it. It's not the same as having a survey, but you can view boats listed on Ebay, you don't have to bid based just on the description and pictures. I wouldn't bid on anything I hadn't seen, the camera can lie! If you view it with the owner present and get satisfactory answers to most of the things on the checklist in this book and you're bidding up to half the price similar boats are advertised for through brokers and other sites then you should have plenty left over if you win the auction.

If you've read this book and studied the checklist at the back you'll soon find as you peruse Ebay ads that hardly a one of the descriptions and specifications offered will answer half the questions you want to ask.

If you do think you've found a bargain you can't resist and you win the auction, then have the survey and or an RNLI safety check after you've purchased and use what you've saved to make the boat one hundred per cent before you start travelling. You could still end up with a saving. Preferably have the full survey and the RNLI safety check. If you go to see the boat and the vendor produces a recent survey and can possibly show he's addressed some or all of the concerns raised by the surveyor then you might want to consider a higher maximum bid than half price.

Boats on Ebay aren't all up for auction, some are listed as classified ads, the vendor pays a fee regardless. Whether a boat is listed as being auctioned or whether it's a classified advertisement there is a 'watch' button on the ad. Ebay will advise you when the auction or the classified ad is nearing the end. You can see what the sorts of boats you are interested in are fetching. Very often a boat you've been watching will be unsold and subsequently relisted and you'll receive a message advising you of that fact if you've been watching it. If you've made a note or taken a screenshot, you'll see if it's been relisted at the original price if it's a classified ad, or whether it's dropped a bit. If it has dropped you've got a motivated seller.

With classified advertisements there is also a 'Make An Offer' button in many cases. Don't be afraid to use it so long as you're serious, but if you're going to view the boat as I would very strongly recommend, then you can do your haggling face to face, after going through the checklist and of course you can make the offer subject to survey. If you travel, visit, view and then haggle face to face the vendor might take you more seriously than if you just use the make an offer button. If you're going to pay for a survey the vendor must put in writing that the boat is off the market until after the survey and your first refusal, and in fairness you of course should put down a deposit.

Most marinas these days have boats in them for sale and some marinas have their own brokerage. In fact some marinas insist clients who want to sell their boats MUST use the marina broker in the terms and conditions for having a berth there. This seems pretty immoral to me, if you own a boat and you're paying for a berth I think that should be quite enough, of course you should behave responsibly, but in my view you shouldn't be told how to sell it, or who can work on it but some marinas are quite arrogant like that.

Anyhow, if you live near a marina or marinas, go take a look. Don't be afraid to travel, I was in Tunbridge Wells when I bought my boat and the boats I surveyed were one up the east coast, one on the south coast and one in Ireland. I viewed boats in a few other locations too. It took ten months from making an absolute decision to change my life and having the money available before I became a boat owner.

Personally I'd fly to Spain, France Greece, whatever if I thought I was on to the right boat and was genuinely interested. Better that than risk buying unseen, I can't imagine being so rash. Not everyone will do so, therefore, once again the vendor has to take you seriously and won't want to lose you.

If you want to sail in the Mediterranean, starting there, as mentioned before, is no hardship and you might get a better deal than in England or the USA. If you do visit marinas to look at boats, look at the marina facilities, prices and terms and conditions while you are there.

The boat you buy might have a few months left on the mooring, or marina, make sure it is transferable. Make a decision as to where you are going to base yourself to begin with, which may be where the boat is at the time of purchase, or it may be elsewhere. Some boats are not in marinas, basins or yards at all but are on swinging moorings in a river or estuary and are accessed by dinghy. For the first weeks or months you'll be wanting to live on board and get to know how things work and make changes. A swinging mooring is cheap but not ideal for your purposes. You may want a parking spot so you can transport things to your new home from the old one.

I joined the sailing club at Gravesend in order to use the canal basin next to the River Thames. It was cheap, relatively speaking, no restrictions on working on the boat myself and plenty of other sailors who also weren't landed gentry or blue blazer and gold button types to help and advise.

You'll need to consider your starting point quite carefully, some marinas have lift out facilities and boatyards, others don't. At Gravesend there are no such facilities but the club members pay for a crane to come and lift all who want it just before winter and put them back just after winter. I arrived mid winter and stayed in the water until I went up to South Dock marina in London. In Chapter 14 we'll talk more about marinas, harbours, moorings and anchorages.

To summarise, although magazines are available initial research is mostly online, Google, Apolloduck, ybw, Ebay and other sites which you'll find by searching. Look at several boats, some will be as advertised, some won't, some will make a nice home, some won't, some will be dry, some wet, some clean, some not so, go and look however tempting the photos, which in common with dating site pictures might be a few years out of date! Some will be fully equipped, others lacking in essential or desirable inventory.

Take the check list, if you're really happy after the viewing and it's an auction then bid by all means, but bid low and be prepared to have a survey and safety check afterwards and to do what's necessary. I would suggest that as well as filling out the checklist that you take photos or make a video when you do viewings and don't muddle them up later! Having something to refer back to when you've looked at a dozen boats and thoroughly confused yourself is a good policy. If you don't win at auction there'll always be another in the pipeline. Decide on your maximum price for any given boat and stick to it, don't get downhearted it IS a buyer's market.

Good Luck.

Scant days after writing this chapter and there's a newspaper story about a couple who bought a multi million pound 'yacht' at a police auction for under £70,000 and now plan to 'sail the world'. The truth emerges if you read on but British newspapers love to sensationalise, especially in headlines. The yacht is a huge motor yacht with two enormous engines and numerous guest rooms, what I'd call a gin palace. The previous owner was convicted of fraud and the yacht seized to help pay off his debts or the cost of prosecution. However it had been left for fifteen years and needed a full restoration which cost the couple a reported £300,000. The article then revealed the yacht has been valued, presumably for insurance at £400,000 leaving what I call a paper profit of between £30,000 and £40,000. I say a paper profit because to realise it they'd have to sell the yacht for £400,000 and that may or may not happen in this market. In the meantime £40,000 will quickly disappear in marina fees, insurance, maintenance and if they visit the Mediterranean as proposed in fuel. However if the couple, now living aboard, are both able to pursue their careers and have made themselves mortgage free it might turn out to be a very good move. I wish them well. Search for these kinds of auctions, there are many different scenarios. Drug runners will often run a very large, powerful and fast expensive rib up on a beach disappear with the cargo and abandon it. It's part of the cost of the operation, the police often this happens in Spain then impound it and later sell it to help the fight against drugs, it's a bizarre world. That's not the kind of boat we're looking for of course. However yachts have been used for smuggling and been caught and impounded. Look for the auctions and not just in the UK. You never know what might come up.

CHAPTER 10
QUALIFICATIONS AND INSURANCE

This book is intended for people dreaming about living on a boat who are unsure how to start. I already knew how sails worked having raced sailing dinghies from a very young age, I'd also sailed with my mother on a 22ft yacht and again with her on larger chartered yachts, so I knew what I was letting myself in for even though I had no formal qualifications.

You'll know if you have any personal experience yourself and can make your decisions accordingly, but let's assume you're completely new to any kind of sailing. Your first step in my view should be to take an RYA dinghy sailing course. This will teach you how sails work and about tacking, gybing, running, reaches and so on. In addition it's a deal of fun, I hope you don't mind getting a bit wet! In a dinghy you don't have to worry about complicated rigging and everything is small and easy to handle. If you don't understand how sails work after that I should consider a motor boat or passage maker, but I have every confidence that you will get it.

My Day Skipper practical course – very arduous.

After that I would take the RYA Day Skipper theory course, you really should do this before you take the practical course because the practical course will make much more sense to you if you do and you're more likely to pass and get the certificate. So, RYA Day Skipper Theory, then RYA Day Skipper Practical. There are two variations on this qualification, tidal and non tidal. There is hardly any rise and fall of tide in the Mediterranean and the non tidal qualification is really for people who exclusively want to sail there. Even if that appeals to you, you may well want to broaden your horizons later so take the tidal course right off.

If you're a bit nervous about jumping right in with Day Skipper, there is an RYA Competent Crew course which would get you started but you'll need to still take Day Skipper as that has an equivalence with the International Certificate Of Competence, once you've passed Day Skipper theory and practical you can ask the RYA to issue you with an ICC, no new exam needed.

I suggested you go straight to Day Skipper to save you money, nothing in sailing is terribly cheap, but the RYA courses are generally very good value. There are different organisations that offer them, I used one in Dartmouth, one in London and one in Gravesend at the time and repeated a couple of the one day courses I'm coming on to next to keep my partner and proposed crew company. She didn't actually sail with me as she became scared of sailing north to Scotland and beyond, but that's another story for another book.

Whether you start with Day Skipper or Competent Crew you'll get to sail on a real yacht. The one I did my course on had in mast furling and a deep fin keel, so quite different from the yacht I bought, but still, I achieved my purpose. You can buy a boat and sail off without any training whatsoever, no one will physically stop you. There are some quite amusing anecdotes about people who did that thinking they'd just keep the coast on their right hand side and ended up going round and round an island. There are more worrying stories of rescues and RNLI folk putting their lives at risk for people with no idea.

Try to be as responsible as you can. Officially you should get the full Yachtmaster qualification, there's also one called Coastal Skipper which falls between Day Skipper and Yachtmaster. You can do the Yachtmaster in one go and have a long sailing trip to boot, but it will cost you thousands of pounds. It might be irresponsible of me to suggest you do less, but I'll tell you what I did, which is more than many and less than others and you can make your own mind up.

By the way the Day Skipper or Competent Crew practical course, Dartmouth Sailing took people aiming for either qualification on the same trip, will focus your mind on what it's like to sail and you'll find out if you get seasick and whether it passes or doesn't, so do a practical sailing course of some kind before you buy a boat, unless you have prior experience. I hope it won't, but it might change your mind and if so little financial damage done.

So, regarding what I did. I took Day Skipper Tidal theory and practical. I also took my VHF Radio Licence with an RYA school, legally required and I took the radar course, diesel engine maintenance course, first aid course, which should be renewed periodically and the sea survival course, all one day events and all affordable. For sea survival, then once again I hope you don't mind getting wet! It does focus your mind on the difficulties of climbing from the sea into a liferaft and much more besides. I used my Day Skipper qualification to obtain the International Certificate Of Competence.

I didn't take Coastal or Yachtmaster which would have added running fixes and other things which I felt I didn't need but cannot say you shouldn't go for. I bought an ex Royal Navy sextant, a couple of books on celestial navigation and practised with the thing. I was always a few miles out, not like the gps! I bought paper charts for all the areas I would sail to as well as electronic ones and I practised coming alongside barges moored in the Thames and anchoring. At least I thought I understood anchoring, turned out it's an artform and although it's part of the day skipper course they simply cannot spend hours or days on it. See my other book if you want to know about life at anchor.

I bought pilot books for all the places I planned to go and I studied them, they're excellent and tell you how to call up marinas, hazards, lines of approach the lot. I always made a passage plan with ports of refuge and waypoints but again this isn't a book about how to sail. What qualifications you take, that's your decision, I'm happy with the way things worked out for me and the amounts I spent.

The Day Skipper Course includes some really useful publications which remind you what various signals and flags mean, what sounds to make with your fog horn in fog, pan pan and mayday radio procedure and lots of other really, really useful stuff. I always kept them handy, anyone can forget and even Yachtmasters have sunk yachts. A certificate is all well and good, but it's what you do, will determine outcomes.

If you want to take fare paying customers you should take the full Yachtmaster and other things like first aid in order to add a commercial endorsement and you should tell your insurer.

Coming on to insurance, when I shopped around and gave my experience and qualifications I had no problems getting insurance. Having a survey and making an undertaking to deal with the points raised helped and when a tourist boat motored into my boat and broke my wind generator and backstay I was able to successfully claim. Although the culprit did not pay up, my insurers did. Spanish tourist boat, on home turf just for the record. Which is why the insurers didn't want to try the courts I suspect.

After a few years, or if you change insurer you may be asked to get a new survey. Ten year old standing rigging is something you'll be expected to renew (unless you have free standing carbon fibre masts on your Freedom 35!). As stated previously you're unlikely to get comprehensive insurance on a Ferro Cement boat, so if that's important to you as it was to me avoid buying such a boat. If you're happy to take the risk, your choice. You really must have third party cover, marinas will normally ask to see it. If you were to damage someone else's boat and you didn't have it things could get messy, expensive and very difficult if you're in some far flung place and don't speak the language so have it and preferably fully comprehensive, you'll get a better level of service as a rule.

In the UK your insurance will normally include a cruising range, most sailors base themselves in a marina and take holidays and trips, as a travelling liveaboard gypsy you'll be one of a substantial minority, but still a minority. When I asked my insurer to extend my insurance to the Baltic AND the Mediterranean in the same year, eyebrows were raised. Nonetheless they did it with the caveat that I got south of the Bay Of Biscay by the end of September after leaving the Herrang Dance Camp in the northern Baltic that summer. I made it and in fact stopped at Singes on the west coast of Portugal for a break then carried on around the Algarve and into the Mediterranean later that winter.

My insurance difficulties started when I wanted to go to the Black Sea. It's not a common destination and insurers are scared to cover you. I needed that certificate to show to the authorities and found a company that would cover me. After I left the Black Sea I stayed with them out of loyalty in return, which was a huge mistake.

The company involved called itself Northern Reef, or North Reef they may have subtly changed the name over time, they had offices in Spain and the UK, I don't know what the current situation is.

When I returned to the UK I stayed at Gallions Reach Marina on the Thames, their website said they had 24 hour CCTV and a 24 hour security guard, in fact they did not. After 5pm no guard and the CCTV didn't function at all. Again I cannot comment on the current setup. After visiting supposedly dangerous places in the Black Sea, the Middle East, North Africa, my boat was comprehensively burgled at Gallions and the insurance company turned out to be dishonest at best totally fraudulent at worst. I say that after talking to the police, see below.

I lost over £6000 worth of possessions, mementoes from my travels and gifts for other people.

The UK police were totally disgraceful, the ombudsman and fraud squad said they could do nothing about the insurance which they believed to be fraudulent, because the head office was in Spain and they believed the owner lived in South America. This despite the company having an office in the UK at least at that time. I'm just relating my personal experiences, but be careful.

I could detail why and how the UK police were so bad and witter on about it but that's not the point. I emailed the Spanish ombudsman, no reply. I posted online, on forums and other places and have been contacted by other people who've been victims of the same insurance company. I've not heard of anyone getting a satisfactory result other than a couple of forum post rebuttals probably made by the company. Hopefully you'll learn from my experience and stick with large well known reputable companies, and that is the point, although what you'll do if you wish to visit the Black Sea I cannot say.

In conclusion third party insurance is essential and I know at least one friend who just lives with that. Comprehensive insurance is very desirable in my view. Initially I used an insurance broker called Yachtmaster and they were good as far as things went. Maybe I should have stuck with them but hindsight isn't twenty twenty.

If you're planning to live this lifestyle for many years then sooner or later your insurers will ask you for a new survey. If the surveyor is part of a firm that does yacht repairs and maintenance beware, they may be looking to make work for themselves. Even if the surveyor is as straight as a die, different surveyor's see things differently, so something your first surveyor was entirely happy with might be condemned by the next one, which is galling, especially if it's been working satisfactorily for years. Thing is, if you've travelled thousands of miles you can't go back to the original surveyor. If this happens you'll just have to bite the bullet.

If you want comprehensive insurance you'll need plenty of budget put aside for when the next survey and or the next standing rigging replacement becomes due. Make sure you have a bit of money behind you and an income if at all possible.

Insurance is a minefield in other ways. The Black Sea isn't the only place it can be tricky to get cover, when you want to cross an ocean you might have fun getting the extension. I have some sympathy with the insurers, but not a whole lot.

It's true that sailing around the UK, or along the coast of France, Spain etc there's a safe harbour roughly every twenty to forty miles and you'll always be sailing with an up to date weather forecast, quite different from a passage lasting weeks, where you have to take what you get. However, sailing around the UK is quite difficult with huge rise and fall of tides in some places and concurrent currents if you'll pardon my French. Some ports dry out so you have to make sure you arrive when there is sufficient water.

Furthermore, all the hazards are close to shore, shallow water, sand banks that shift, rocks awash, then there's traffic, fishing boats, cargo, tourist boats, ferries not so many of those in mid Atlantic. You're not likely to hit anything mid ocean, it can happen, don't take it for granted, but it's much more likely once you get close to land. Waves can be huge in the deep mid Atlantic but they're not as threatening generally as they are in the shallow North Sea for example that pushes them up good and steep. In fact you could sail over a Tsunami mid ocean because it's the rising seabed close to land that pushes it up, as it does Atlantic waves arriving in Portugal. I've seen huge ships disappear completely from view there.

If you can't get cover for the crossing itself you might well be able to get cover from the time you arrive a certain distance offshore, or at least for marinas and ports etc. Ocean crossings make weather forecasts pretty meaningless, but you reduce the risk by travelling at the right time of year and books are available for Atlantic and Pacific crossings. You're swapping one set of risks for others, but insurers still don't entirely like it very often.

Using an insurance broker means you have more clout in a way, the broker places a lot of business and the actual insurer may want to be helpful accordingly.

Next we'll have a chat about navigation equipment, it's not just about gps.

CHAPTER 11
NAVIGATION EQUIPMENT

My boat came with this antiquated, but functioning chart plotter, the two handhelds I purchased subsequently offered far more features and accepted far more detailed charts. To the left is the control for the autopilot which controlled a powerful hydraulic ram connected to the rudder, it couldn't cope with a hurricane but was very, very impressive most of the time, behind that is a depth sounder/fishfinder, quite hi tech at the time. Navigation wise an iPad will do almost anything these days and if you need to change electronics they're one of the few things that have become less expensive with progress.

The obvious piece of navigation equipment is a gps, these days that generally means a gps chart plotter that will show a picture of the chart for the area you are in and show precisely where you are on that chart. It's a marvellous piece of technology. The charts maybe loaded into it by a kind of cassette or they may be a paid download from the internet. Some yachtsmen I've encountered have pirated copies of charts supplied for commercial shipping I'm not suggesting you should seek to get your hands on those.

What you should do is to find out what charts come with the boat, is it UK and Ireland only or are there charts for the whole world at the other end of the spectrum. The boat I bought had a very early chart plotter and the charts supplied with it for Ireland and Norway primarily were very basic to say the least, with very little of the detail you'd see on printed charts. Ask for a demonstration from the vendor.

I purchased a hand held chart plotter and when that started giving problems I bought another, although the first was later sorted out. Hand held plotters are great you can take them outside on deck if you have an outside steering position and then you can use your first piece of navigation equipment, your eyes, at the same time as seeing what the depth should be and that you're on the right track and so on. The only downside to hand held plotters is tat back then the screen was quite small.

Back then it was also possible to load charts on a laptop and buy a receiver one could plug in to show your position on said chart. I had some difficulty setting it up, but another yachttie helped me get that working too. That particular computer was stolen in London but I still have the two handhelds and all my cassettes. I preferred cassettes over downloads, because I figured if the download fails or gets interrupted I might lose my purchase, big companies aren't always known for their trust or regard for customers and I imagine some customers try to rip them off too. I once lost some video editing software that way.

Cassettes of course can be plugged into another matching machine if the first machine should fail. I purchased my first hand held and the cassettes I needed at the Southampton Boat Show and added cassettes for other regions as I travelled. I can't remember the prices but they weren't cheap and I don't suppose they've got cheaper, although the actual hardware may well have got cheaper as tech often does.

I kept my cassettes in three watertight bags, just to be sure! You don't want the tiny contacts getting corroded so watertight, airtight storage is a good idea I feel. What matters when you buy the boat is what does it come with. These days electronics aren't the biggest bill you might face, but charts are valuable and the age of those charts matters. Just as a SatNav for your car can have out of date maps so a chart plotter can have out of date charts. If you have an up to date Pilot Book for the places you're going it might not be the end of the world, but sandbanks can shift, harbour entrances can be re-modelled, even mistakes on the chart get rectified occasionally. The more up to date your charts the better.

When I made my last delivery trip the yacht owner had all the charts downloaded via the internet on to an ipad tablet. Great idea, he'd downloaded the charts at home over a secure connection, the ipad has a built in gps receiver of course and like the handhelds could be charged on board the boat. Now you have a handheld with a big screen. Stick some velcro on it and you can mount it in the wheelhouse too. It's worth checking what sockets are available and how the vendor charges things like laptops and tablets. It's good to be able to do that at sea. Inverters are available but you should not have to convert the voltage to mains voltage and back down again, it is possible to have the kind of cigarette lighter 12v socket you get in a car and most mobiles, tablets etc have a charger for those as well as for mains. See what the vendor has, an inverter is sometimes useful to have especially if you restrict yourself to using it to only when the engine is running.

A gps chart plotter is not the only piece of navigation equipment you'll want to have, as superb as they are, they'll give you speed over the ground and show your direction accurately and the more you use it the more features you'll discover.

However you need a depth sounder, a sonar, preferably pointing forward a bit. Know your draft and know where the sensor is mounted on the hull, it's going to be below the water, but not at the bottom of the keel. You can normally calibrate the thing and make allowance that the boat is deeper than the sensor. Best thing is to make a plumb line check accurately the depth and calibrate accordingly. I made a plumb line from some narrow, strong white tape and marked it up with indelible marker I then calibrated my depth sounders, the boat actually came with two an old fashioned NASA and a nice modern sonar with a screen that was also a fish finder.

You can either calibrate it so it gives the depth of water from the surface, which should correspond with the chart once you've allowed for tide, or you can calibrate it in such a way that the reading represents the depth of water below your keel. Either is acceptable, so long as you remember. I call it a piece of navigation equipment because if the charted depth and the reading you're getting differ greatly, then you're not where you think you are and need to start working out what's going on pronto.

Binoculars are a vital piece of navigation equipment, not expensive so if the vendor is not leaving a pair, buy some. The best you can. Many for sailors have a built in compass and will give you a bearing on a landmark. A normal hand held compass for sailing will also allow you to take a bearing and you should have one, but binoculars allow you to get a bearing on something that's further off, so get binoculars that have that feature I'd say.

Your boat should have a compass built in. In these days of chart plotters you may not need it so much, but once again if you lose your chart plotter you may want it. I wouldn't go to sea without several chart plotters. The one built into the boat is not much good without an electrical supply, so if there's a failure.... My first hand held used AA batteries, so I always kept a good supply in a watertight place. My second newer handheld had a rechargeable Lithium battery, I bought a spare battery for that, used both batteries and kept them healthy and charged.

Nonetheless, if you lose the lot a compass will help you sail in an appropriate direction, if you can't use the sun or stars. Your compass should be swung. The compass built into your boat won't necessarily be one hundred percent accurate. Swinging the compass means turning the boat through 360 degrees and working out the errors and how they change as you rotate. It's a bit of an art. At the time I read up about it and did it myself. I won't be trying to explain it here, but the boat you buy will probably have a built in compass and knowing that it's accurate and what the errors are is important. Ask the vendor, has the compass been swung recently by someone who knew what they were doing and where are the results?

Steel boats tend to suffer greater inaccuracies than fibreglass or wooden boats but there are still things on board that can interfere with the compass. The magnetic field of the earth is changing too. Some scientists believe the polarity was once reversed and may change again. Did you know that the earth has a magnetic field due to its molten core and that if the core was to cool sufficiently and solidify we'd lose both our magnetic field and our atmosphere. Makes you think doesn't it!

Anyway, magnetic north and true north are not the same thing and depending where you are on the globe the affect of this could be more, could be less. Your paper charts will tell you what the variance is, so long as they are up to date.

That deals with gps, depth and compass. Your radar can show you the contours of the land when in range, by the way you can alter the range of your radar, up to whatever it's maximum is, depending n the model. Radar is not essential but as I've said before it is highly desirable and this is one of the reasons. If chart and depth don't agree and you're trying to puzzle it out radar might help. As might calling a friend so regard your radio as part of your armoury.

When I was skydiving we carried altimeters, but anything made by man can fail, so another way of knowing how high you were was to count seconds, not as accurate as a stopwatch so some people carried those, another was to see what those around you were doing, if all those around you were opening parachutes and your altimeter said ten thousand feet still I'd follow the example of the others! The final altimeter was the mark 1 eyeball, if the ground looked too close it probably was!

Your boat likewise has an armoury of things to help you be sure where you are, and whether there's sufficient water underneath you. Get used to using them all. Most skydivers only carry one altimeter, but you have room for several plotters with different types of power supply, even your mobile phone can usually give you a Latitude and Longitude you can then plot on a paper chart. Paper charts still have a place, what does your boat come with?

Flying a Greek courtesy flag under the spreader in Greek waters; try not to forget or to make sure you have them in advance and not too tatty either, especially in Turkey, people tend to get upset, particularly the authorities and for goodness sake don't fly the Greek one in Turkish waters or vice versa, the border between the two can be close in the islands!

It's not strictly navigation, but when you enter the territorial waters of another country you'll need to fly a courtesy flag from your spreaders, does the boat come with a good selection or has it stayed in UK waters? I inherited about thirty! You'll also need a Q or quarantine flag if you're entering a place where you need to clear customs, it's just a plain yellow flag, if there isn't one on board you can buy or make one before you travel.

I carried a recently calibrated sextant and an old fashioned trailing log, like a propeller on the end of a line which you tow and which at the boat end tells you your speed through the water. I never used either in anger and now they're just mementoes. Carrying a sextant, you can buy plastic ones quite cheaply, might be reassuring, but you'll have to get a book on celestial navigation and practise both using it and the arithmetic need to actually give you a latitude and longitude that you can then mark on a chart. Like me you'll never get anywhere near the accuracy of a gps.

Charts are generally for close to land, for fun I carried a Times Atlas of the world which had the lat and long marked at the side and top/bottom of the pages. Just for fun though. If the satellites ever get turned off it probably means nuclear war, and then the best place to be, is lost at sea!

CHAPTER 12
SAFETY EQUIPMENT, TENDERS, BACKUPS AND SPARE EVERYTHING

The list of safety equipment is quite long and much of it you might want to buy after you've bought the boat, but if it comes with good quality, up to date equipment such as a new or not very old liferaft that's been kept serviced and in date then that is certainly a plus. Lifejackets don't want to be too old either, nor horseshoe life rings, danbuoys, safety harnesses, etc.

Let's start with the liferaft. Most liferafts come in a hard shell and are mounted on deck or possibly are attached to the stern rail. Some cheaper ones come in a soft container, I'd prefer one in a hard protective shell. They are supposed to be serviced every few years and it is essential they are. However well protected, sea water might have got in. Boats move around, something might have chafed. Hidden inside the liferaft are a very few essentials to keep you alive including some fresh water. It should be sealed but having the liferaft checked and re-victualled every so often is eminently sensible.

Quiz the vendor, see the receipts. Although I'm getting off the subject of boat buying yet again, just for a moment, people who do blue water sailing should carry grab bags. A grab bag is a waterproof container, with enough air in it to ensure it floats.

The idea is that if your boat sinks you grab said grab bag or bags and chuck them in the liferaft. If you miss they should float! As well as air they should have more bottled water and anything else you might find that could help you to survive. I'd include a hand held radio and spare battery, something to get a fix, ideally a hand held plotter and batteries, chocolate and other high energy foods, flares, binoculars, a knife and fishing gear but do be careful how you use such items in an inflatable, even a cell phone, you never know, you might drift close enough to land to get a signal. Mine also had an inflatable solar still. This will turn seawater into freshwater, very slowly and in small quantities, but they're compact, lightweight and easy to add to your liferaft. I'll be talking about EPIRBs in a moment but if you have a personal EPIRB, make sure it goes with you.

I kept a couple of large water containers with handles near my grab bags, but far from full so they'd float and be light enough to haul into the raft if they'd gone into the sea.

I carried a horseshoe lifering with automatic light on each side of the aft deck, the yellow bag to the right holds a floating line, part of the man overboard recovery system and to the left you can see part of the Danbuoy.

See how the liferaft is attached, it should have an automatic release, but you want to know how to do it yourself, just in case, don't enter the water and wait for the liferaft to appear, it might get stuck. It is possible to carry a search and rescue transponder, which will show up on the radar screen of a big ship. If you have one in your liferaft and a lightweight telescopic carbon fibre mast you can mount it on it too could be a lifesaver. I carried on but I think these days most people rely on EPIRB and or SatPhone, still it's not a big thing to carry.

Steel yachts show up well on radar as a rule, wooden and fibreglass boats less well. Even so I carried a thing called a radar reflector high in my rigging. See if the boat you are buying has one, if not, add it to your shopping list.

The blue line running across the porthole is part of the boat's safety harness for clipping on to when doing things out on deck whilst at sea.

Other inventory the boat might come with, horseshoe life rings, they'll be in fittings on a handrail normally, the sun degrades them, look at the condition. Likewise there should be a Danbuoy you can throw to a person who's gone overboard, it has a weight well below the float and a tall rod with a flag on it. Looks a bit like a fishing float. Not losing sight of a small head in the water when someone is overboard is very, very hard a Danbuoy with its flag just a few feet above the water makes it much easier.

A properly equipped blue water yacht will have a safety harness made of tough webbing running fore and aft and with a section across where necessary, it should be routed so it's easy to clip on to, but is not a tripping hazard, so flat on the floor or along the cabin sides. I had a new one made by a friend who's a parachute rigger, again, the sun degrades things like this. You should not be clipping on to a wire hand rail, you have to unclip every time you come to a stanchion and they're not designed for the purpose.

Lifejackets which inflate when immersed in water are more comfortable and less bulky than older types or dinghy type life jackets. They should also have legstraps and constitute a safety harness. Because they have gas bottles and something to set the gas off when wet, they need to be kept dry if at all possible and like your liferaft they need to be checked periodically and serviced. Safety lines that connect your harness or lifejacket, to the harness of the boat are essential items of inventory. They need to be long enough to allow movement, short enough not to tangle easily or trip. There are elasticated ones which I like I must say. They have a large metal hook at each end that snaps on and will slide along the boat harness. They snap on and lock but be aware they can, very rarely, come undone.

A harness for you personally is an option, less bulky than a lifejacket and if you don't go overboard you don't need a lifejacket. I used mine quite a lot. Sailing solo no one was going to stop the boat, turn it around and come pick me up so, not going overboard was key.

The boat you buy should have a man overboard recovery system. Again, it won't help you when you're solo but it might save a friend or loved one, or you yourself if you have someone else on board in an emergency who's competent. I rigged one up on a pulley permanently attached to my main boom in such a place that the line could go to one of the winches on either side of the wheelhouse with the boom swung out and locked in place by the gybe controller. A fully dressed person saturated with seawater with sailing gear and a lifejacket is heavy, very heavy, no matter how slightly built.

Floating lines, ie floating ropes a person can grab a hold of are a useful part of a boat's inventory in my opinion but the two most important items in your safety set up are the liferaft and the EPIRB. You could, I suppose, substitute a SatPhone, for an EPIRB, but you won't be making phone calls anytime you're alive but unconscious. If I had a SatPhone I still wouldn't go to sea without an EPIRB.

What's an EPIRB? It stands for Electronic Position Indicating Radio Beacon. My boat came with one, but the one I had is now useless as the frequency it operated on is no longer used. As mentioned earlier you can have one registered to the boat or to you personally. By the end of my decade I had both.

An EPIRB, once activated sends a message, with your position to a Satellite. The mayday message is then sent to a listening station, one in the northern hemisphere, one in the southern. They will identify you from the registration and if it applies to the yacht they'll know what type and colour of yacht they are looking for. My EPIRB was on the wheelhouse roof with a release system the same as that for the liferaft, if the boat sank, the EPIRB should automatically bob to the surface and start transmitting. Ideally you'd activate it before things got that bad and ensure you don't get separated from it. It is permissible to activate it before the boat is lost and the yacht is easier to spot than a liferaft. It is NOT permissible to activate it unless lives are genuinely at risk.

If you activate it accidentally you're supposed to let them know, which from a marina is not so difficult, from mid ocean you'd need that SatPhone. Like going overboard there are some things you really should guard against, very, very carefully.

My liferaft is in the hard white plastic case in front of the main mast, the little thing front centre on the shell is the automatic release which has a date marked on it by which time it must be replaced. The small rectangular box between the solar panels on the wheelhouse roof is the EPIRB, which has a similar automatic release. You can also see my passerelle, an old scaffold board, this is before I fitted wheels to it although the holes have been drilled for the cross piece.

The listening station will alert the nearest air sea rescue to your location, which depending on where you are in the world could be excellent or less so. However as a system it is a wondrous thing. If you have a small, personal EPIRB registered to you, you can of course take it off piste skiing, mountaineering, tracing the Amazon, pick your adventure!

We've now discussed the main points relating to safety equipment on board, as always don't be afraid to quiz the vendor or broker, or both as appropriate.

Another aspect to safety is back ups. My boat came with hydraulic steering, it had a great big hydraulic ram inboard, at the stern above the rudder. It also had a tunnel above the rudder, a sort of large vertical steel tube with a watertight hatch on top so you could inspect a jammed rudder without diving. (Beginning to wonder why I sold the damn thing!) As a back up to the hydraulic steering it had chains and cables. In addition to that there was a ring welded to the top of the rudder, this would allow a line to be attached and led to the winches on each side of the wheelhouse, to turn the rudder that way. As if all that weren't enough I had pintels welded on to the stern and a rudder custom made to fit with a tiller that rose up above the aft deck.

The RNLI safety inspector actually told me I was too careful and had too many backups. However the first two backups would have moved the existing rudder. If the rudder had been lost, or jammed solid, my tiller and spare rudder would have allowed me to steer. It's very difficult to sail or motor if you cannot steer. I heard about a yacht whose rudder became jammed hard one way in the Atlantic. Unable to do anything but go around in circles they issued a Mayday, however, because they were afloat with ample food and water they were judged to not be in mortal danger and were not picked up until they drifted into a shipping lane some weeks later. Stories one hears in marinas could be true, part true or pure fiction, but steering is essential either way.

Bilge pumps and gas alarms we've already touched on, it's also possible to have a bilge water alarm fitted, which is fine when you're there but automatic pumps are vital if you're not there. Boats have been known to spring a leak and sink in a marina, the staff at the marina should be alert and competent to save it, but don't bank on it, if your boat drags down their pontoon or damages other boats as it sinks they're more likely to invoice you.

Automatic bilge water pumps are electric and have a float, if the float rises due to incoming water on they go. They take their power from the domestic supply as a rule. You should also be able to turn them on regardless of the position of the float. Make sure if the bilge is compartmentalised that there is at least one for each compartment and at least three spread out through the boat. Here is another reason to have a bullet proof electrical system, there's a useful book entitled the twelve volt bible. When you leave your boat consider how you're going to leave it. With your four way switch you should be able to leave the domestic supply on and nothing else.

You might think to leave the boat plugged into shore power in a marina when you leave the boat, especially if it's part of your fee. However other sailors might unplug you because they want the socket, the marina staff might unplug you thinking you're being greedy plugging in when you're not there. These things happen. Even the owner of an aluminium yacht might unplug a steel yacht because he's worried about electrolytic corrosion. You can't take anything for granted.

I left my boat unplugged with domestic batteries on, the solar panels clean and uncovered, the wind generator free to turn. Make sure your bilges are clean, if the pumps come on it's because they need to, if debris, dirt, paper, rust or anything at all clogs them up, they simply stop working. So be careful what if anything you store in the bilges. You'll also want your boat to have manual bilge pumps, these can very often clear more water and faster, but you have to keep pumping. One for each compartment. See what is there when you view and check it works if possible. Most electric bilge pumps clip into a kind of filter, you can pull them out for cleaning. If you carry spares of the exact same model, you can swap them quickly and easily, without removing the cradle they sit in.

You won't find this on any inventory I've ever seen, but I offer it as a thought something I decided on for myself. I carried an electric 240 volt submersible pump of the sort used to clear flooded drains and ditches or empty ponds. I never needed it, maybe the RNLI guy was right about all my backups, but I believe in personal responsibility. You'll get tired after a few hours on a hand pump. My 240 volt pump from a well known tool supplier could be plugged straight into my portable petrol generator. The petrol will run out eventually but, it'll clear a lot of water quickly and independently of the yacht's systems which might have failed.

Not least amongst your safety concerns is fire, there is no fire brigade offshore and although a lifeboat or the coastguard might be able to hose you down, if they arrive in time, they're more concerned with saving lives than property.

Different types of fire extinguisher are for different types of fire, water on an electrical fire does not help as a general rule. There are automatic fire extinguishers with expensive gasses which can be, and should be, fitted within your engine bay. They're expensive, they have a gauge to show the pressure has not gone down and they have a life expectancy after which they should be renewed. See what the boat comes with, or again add it to your shopping list. The good news is that engine bays are a relatively small space, fill it with gas and choke off the oxygen and a fire will normally be put out quite quickly. Diesel is, thankfully not explosive like petrol. Be careful where you store the petrol for outboards and generators, mine was outside.

You should have at least one fire extinguisher in each cabin, I used dry powder, well never actually used them, but carried them, they also have a gauge to show they are still under pressure. However I'm told the powder can settle and solidify. They're not expensive, change them every couple of years. You should also have a fire blanket near the cooker and a smoke alarm. A fire could start while you're asleep. In fact I was at an anchorage in Spain when a boat caught fire during the night and subsequently exploded and sank. The couple on board escaped but were hospitalised.

Most yachts won't have two engines with the exception of the majority of catamarans. Some of those only have one central engine or use an outboard but the majority large enough to live on will have an engine and transmission in each hull. You're not likely to find a monohull yacht with two engines. Passage makers are obliged to if they're a true passage maker, it can be a wing engine, smaller and off to the side but it must have it's own independent transmission and propeller.

Most of us yachties carry an outboard or even two. I had a bracket welded on to the stern of my yacht so that I could use an outboard. A friend of mine used a four horsepower outboard to manoeuvre his huge barge in still water. An outboard and a small can of petrol won't give you much range, but if you sail close to a port or marina and no one answers the radio, you can get in and manoeuvre with it.

Spares for anything easily replaced should be carried, rigging spares, engine spares, electrical spares, bulbs, pumps, plumbing, wooden bungs, sails. If the vendor advertises the yacht as a liveaboard see just what he's done and where he's been, if he's led the lifestyle we're discussing here, he should be well equipped – what is he leaving on board?

I also carried a crowbar and bolt cutters, if a mast comes down and is in the sea on one side, well, it's only likely to happen in rough conditions so it's potentially fatal, you have to get rid of it and fast hence the bolt cutters and crowbar. Bolt cutters will go through wire standing rigging like a hot knife through butter. A really good quality, sharp knife that will cut through tough ropes as opposed to wire rigging should also be mounted somewhere close to where you sail from, ie wheelhouse or cockpit, somewhere where you can grab it in an instant. If you are worried about intruders getting their hands on said knife, highly unlikely in most marinas, then take it out when you go to bed or are based somewhere for a period. Security in anchorages is discussed in my other sailing book, bad people have been known to swim out to yachts at anchor, swimmers don't make much noise and the stories are terrifying, but thankfully very very rare.

I have met sailors carrying firearms, or a crossbow, catapult, ball bearing gun, speargun. The last is likely to be legal, but not very effective above water except at very close range and it takes time to load. Not wanting to get into trouble with the authorities I think the best policy is just to be careful where you go and how you conduct yourself. I've heard of American sailors with automatic weapons fighting off pirates, but generally pirates will be better equipped than you are. Sadly there are some places I just wouldn't go now and the pirates are venturing far out to sea in certain areas.

Wooden bungs of a variety of sizes I carried under the sink. They can plug a through hull fitting or a pipe that's come astray and is spurting water. The wood expands when it gets wet to make a firm seal. You need a variety of sizes and to keep them dry until they are ever needed. I carried a sail repair kit and all sorts of tapes and glues, the sail repair kit had a range of needles and saddler's palm a device you slip over your thumb to help you push a strong needle through tough fabric. A repair kit for your inflatable should also be carried assuming you have an inflatable tender.

So the next essential for this lifestyle is in fact a dinghy, or tender. Same thing. A boat like a MacGregor can get right into the beach, so doesn't really need a tender and isn't designed to carry one, it would have to be deflated on deck or towed, but a MacGregor isn't my ideal liveaboard. I'd want something bigger. Catamarans can get very close in and usually take the ground, but then you're vulnerable to thieves and a catamaran can easily transport a dinghy, and anchor off where it is less vulnerable to criminals.

Some yachtsmen do keep their tender deflated and tied down on deck, but then you have to pump it up every time you want to use it. Another option is to tow it but marinas prefer it's not taking up space on the water as a general rule. Some are more enlightened and it can be fun to use it in the marina to visit friends rather than possibly having to walk right around.

Look for a boat with davits, those are the two frames hanging over the stern with lines and pulleys that enable you to raise a dinghy. Not essential but very, very desirable. You want a board bolted or welded onto the handrail near the stern ideally which you can attach your outboard motor to. The davits don't want to carry the excess weight of a dinghy with the outboard still attached, especially in a rough sea. I had one board for mounting an outboard motor on each side and a spare outboard but you know me by now. I had a spare tender too!

My plastic tender would actually get up on a plane with only me aboard and with a five horsepower outboard. The main advantage was it couldn't easily be vandalised or damaged on rocks, nor could it be deflated and put in the boot of a car, there was even a built in locking compartment for odds and ends.

A word of caution lock up your outboards they're very attractive to the light fingered and lock up your tender too. Sometimes at anchor, or on a mooring I'd leave the tender on the water attached to the boat, to make commuting ashore to shop or sightsee quicker and easier, but it was chained and padlocked to the yacht. A length of stainless chain is very useful if you don't want your tender rust stained, or your clothes come to that. I know of tenders being stolen in Sicily and Malta, it's not common but then I had one wrecked once in Spain as well, outboard thefts are reported all over the place, even sailing clubs and marinas, so the bad guys are out there.

I have seen catamarans, having the dinghy attached to the davits with the outboard still on the stern of the dinghy. If the davits are strong enough and given catamarans are very stable, all well and good, but I wouldn't cross an ocean with that lot dangling at the back.

Consider what kind of tender you are looking for. Basically the smaller the yacht the smaller the tender, there are some very small inflatables indeed. Two people max. The cheapest inflatables have a fabric floor stiffened with battens. Others have a fabric floor but with a full flat wooden floor as well and others are ribs as mentioned earlier, rigid inflatable boats. These have a proper v shaped plastic hull set into the tubes and can get up on a plane with the right outboard making long journeys practical and rapid, and some anchorages are very large indeed. Take the harbour at Mahon, in Menorca for example, where you might anchor but you'll want a tender with an outboard to go anywhere pretty much. Shopping for example.

My Tinker was pricey but fun. It was once classed as a liferaft too. These days I'd probably look for a Walker Bay to hang on my davits as a tender I could also sail.

My boat came with a Zodiac inflatable, common mid priced brand, fabric floor with slats in my case and quite old. I figured I'd use it till it dropped. I also bought a brand new Tinker Funsail. The company has gone on to bigger and better things since and new Tinkers aren't available. They were built to a standard, a high standard. Mine was once classed as a liferaft too, before the regs changed. It has four compartments, two inside two, so if an outer puncture occurs that side will still function. As a liferaft back up it had a sea anchor and a canopy. As the name suggests it could sail, it had a rudder, tiller, tiller extension, daggerboard, mast, rigging, mainsail and jib. It also had davit points so it could be hoisted easily. With all those optional extras it cost a fortune. I'm not saying it wasn't value for money I have it still and love it, but it was pricey.

I bought it because I wanted a sailing dinghy along primarily and of course it was yet another backup, this time to my automatic life raft on deck. I never used it as a tender because I became so scared of it getting stolen or vandalised! I did sail it once or twice though.

Why did I become so paranoid. Well, at Fuengirola I'd arranged to meet my daughter, I actually sailed a long way back on myself to keep the appointment and it's the only time in ten years I found a marina so full I couldn't get a spot. It's happened once since on a delivery too, but it's uncommon. As a result I anchored outside the marina, off the beach, not ideal but do-able.

I went ashore in my Zodiac which I chained and padlocked with the chain around and under a huge boulder. The outboard was locked to the transom of the dinghy too. When I came back someone had slashed the Zodiac. Whether they had meant to rob the yacht, or steal the outboard and found they couldn't or were just plain nasty I don't know, but I had to swim back pushing the half inflated tender with my going out clothes in a bundle too whilst trying to keep the working parts of the outboard out of the sea, in quite a swell. A potential recipe for drowning actually, but I got back, got everything aboard somehow and went to bed exhausted. Next day I spent most of the day repairing the knife slash in the Zodiac as I certainly wasn't going to risk the Tinker from that day forth.

I did a good job though I say so myself and it was airtight, but I never again trusted it fully so I kept my eyes open for a bargain tender. In one marina shop in Valencia I saw a plastic dinghy shaped exactly like an inflatable, but made of some kind of polyurethane, white plastic anyway, hanging on the wall. It was half price, presumably they hadn't been able to sell it. It even had plastic wheels to help you bring it up a concrete ramp, or, as in my case, walk it easily back to my boat after I bought it. A similar thing is available in aluminium, at least I've seen them, don't know if they're available new, but they're around.

It was a lot heavier than the Zodiac but well within the capabilities of my steel davits. I couldn't see a knife going through it OR a rock in shallow water come to that. I used it for about eight years and it was great, but I sold it with the yacht and kept the Tinker.

Tied up here in the Caribbean two yacht tenders in front is a typical RIB, behind what looks to me like a Walker Bay dinghy without its optional inflatable tube around the gunwhale. The tube would make it less easy to capsize, but is not essential so as with the plastic tender I bought it's always likely to get you home. The difference is that you can drop a mast into the Walker Bay and do some dinghy sailing.

If I were starting from scratch and my yacht could take one on its davits I'd buy a dinghy called a Walker Bay. It appears to be made from a similar plastic to that of my last tender, but it's a proper little sailing dinghy with a self supporting mast. An inflatable collar is an optional extra, and that's what I'd have. My Tinker hardly ever got sailed because of the time it took to assemble it all. With a Walker Bay one can motor, row or sail, it's got a proper hull like a rib and the safety of an inflatable collar too. However it doesn't rely on the inflatable collar so it's largely safe from vandals. And rocks since the inflatable collar is usually above the water. If it's kept on the davits all one need do is lower it, drop in the mast sails and rudder and sail off.

If your tender is heavy, tie it in every direction possible to save it moving in rough seas, that's the only downside of a rigid type.

When you buy your yacht see what tender comes with it and whether its quick and easy to launch. How robust is it, is the outboard in good order; one can row an inflatable, but an out board is really essential in some anchorages and windy conditions. No tender, no outboard or kit that's on its last legs or appears unsuitable – haggle.

If you row ashore in your tender in light airs and then face a really strong headwind to get home some hours later it can be challenging to say the least.

You'll need fenders to protect the hull from chaffing against harbour walls and if the harbour walls are rough and abrasive enough to burst your fenders you'll need thick wooden boards drilled at each end and with ropes attached to hang between fenders and harbour wall! You'll need good strong warps to tie up and put old hosepipe over them if they're in danger of chafing, they're expensive to replace aside from the risk of the lines breaking with consequences for your boat and those around it.

You may be able to jump on and off your boat like a gazelle, but if you're bows to it's not so easy with shopping and so on and you may have guests who are less fit, so a passerelle or walkway is ideal, you can buy a posh one with a handrail, but I got an old scaffold board, made an attachment for the bow at one end and a cross piece with wheels for the other, to keep it stable and to allow it to move with the boat.

You could add dehumidifiers and al sorts, it's almost never ending, or would be if you had the space. However, I hope that focusses your mind on the kind of onboard equipment you'll need. Don't expect a second hand boat to have everything and certainly not new, but if you're buying from someone who's lived on board and travelled extensively you are actually likely to find a lot of this stuff is already there, unless they're simply moving to a newer, or bigger, or smaller boat. Make sure you know what is staying and what they're taking with them, right down to cutlery and unbreakable plates and glasses!

CHAPTER 13
SURVEYS AND SAFETY CHECKS

A full survey will cost several hundred pounds a survey on a steel yacht even more due to the cost of the ultrasound on the hull. Surveys are done with the boat out of the water, so you have to add the cost of the lift out and the lift back in, also in three figures generally, but varies by marina and country. However you look at it, it's an expensive business.

A reputable surveyor will produce a small book with his findings and recommendations. He cannot tell the age of standing rigging just by looking at it. He should be able to spot broken strands and such like, but much of the time he will do only what you can do yourself and quiz the owner and ask to see receipts and form an opinion, something you also can do.

The thing is there are many other things you cannot do or spot yourself, unless an expert, so a survey is a necessary thing. Preferably before you buy the boat, but if you've bought it cheap at auction have a survey afterwards, you need to know the condition of the hull especially; you can probably ascertain the age of the liferaft from the information on the case and you can ask to see the service record just as the surveyor can. That goes for all sorts of things, you can judge the condition of horseshoe life rings, ask to see when lifejackets were serviced, look for peeling varnish, look for rust in the bilges, see if the engine bay is clean and orderly and on and on. See if things are faded or polished or painted.

Pretty much everything, actually I hope everything, you can ascertain for yourself is on my checklist, but insurers will want a recent survey if they're to give you comprehensive cover. You might think oh I'll just throw it at a boatyard and tell them to do whatever is necessary, but you'd be abrogating responsibility to them, they might just do the jobs that interest them and you still won't have that bit of paper for the insurers, so bite the bullet.

Probably ninety nine times out of a hundred the surveyor won't run the engine because the boat is out of the water. This is a pretty timid excuse in my view since he could get there before the lift out or stay for the lift in. It's possible to rig up cooling water via a hose and readily available fittings. The only type of cooling system that would arguably be a problem would be keel cooling like mine, ie a completely sealed fresh water system with pipes under the boat which should be immersed in the sea, or river, or canal. Even with that system the engine could be run briefly out of the water and turned off before it got hot.

As galling as it is to pay so much for a survey and have a key, vital area ignored, you can probably make as good a judgement as the surveyor would about the engine, and insurers are used to seeing in a surveyor's report that the engine wasn't run and cannot be commented on. When you do your viewing with the boat in the water, have the engine started, see if it starts easily, does it smoke briefly then clean up, is water coming from the exhaust if necessary, does it sound right, we've most of us had diesel cars or know someone who has, we have an idea how it should sound.

Before starting it you can ascertain whether the engine bay is clean and tidy, whether the wiring is all nicely secured and terminals insulated. You can check the oil, it's just a dipstick like a car. Check receipts. Enquire how oil changes are done, I came across one vendor who'd never done one! Just topped it up periodically. Putting all these things together with the impression you form about the knowledge and attitude of the vendor and you'll do alright. Some older yachts are on their second engine, if you're lucky, and it's not that uncommon, you might find a boat for sale with a lovely new, or nearly new, Bukh or Yanmar, in a boat that once had an old taxi engine. It's not so very uncommon.

Before you go travelling an RNLI safety check is a good idea. The RNLI is the Royal National Lifeboat Institution. They have bases all round the UK coast unsurprisingly and in London and on other major rivers. It's a charity, quite a wealthy one by all accounts. I can't remember now what I paid, or whether I made a donation, but it's worth doing if only for your own peace of mind. Call them up and they'll send someone over, prevention is better than cure.

If you get all your ducks in a row first, make sure flares, liferaft, lifejackets, fire extinguishers are all new or serviced, there should be a fire blanket within easy reach near the cooker too, and at least one smoke alarm. It's all on the checklist. Make sure you have a man overboard recovery system that's man enough for the job, have lifelines and a harness to clip on to that's not old and degraded, ensure that everything electrical is in working order on the day of the inspection, you'll end up with a piece of paper, which you could append to the survey when you send it in to your insurer if it's not too late. They don't ask for it, but it shows two things, one that the boat is as safe as possible and two that you have a responsible attitude. The RNLI representative may quiz you too to see that you know what to do in an emergency.

If you've had a survey and a safety check and attended to every issue raised you should be as prepared and safe as it's possible to be. Personally I like to think things through for myself which is why I did things others wouldn't such as the back up rudder and the commercial water pump. Do whatever feels right to you, it's your boat, your life and you may be responsible for the safety of others.

In fact I've written a design brief for what I call a World Explorer Yacht, I'd need a naval architect to turn it into drawings and a boatyard to build it. In short I'd need to win the lottery big time, but I do feel boat safety can be improved, especially if you want to go to icy places or round the capes. Still like me you probably can't run to having a boat built to your specifications, so the above is pretty much all you can do.

Once again, good luck with both survey and safety check.

CHAPTER 14
WHERE WILL I KEEP IT - MARINAS AND ANCHORAGES

Once you start travelling this is a question that will answer itself, you'll be living aboard, travelling from place to place, if you like somewhere you stay a bit longer, if you've exhausted what it has to offer you, you move on, the marina is too expensive you move on, you find a secure, beautiful, free anchorage with access to food shopping, you might choose to stay a while longer than initially planned.

I spent as much of the summer as possible at sea or at anchor. In the Mediterranean especially marina prices are high. It used to be just August, when firms in France and Italy especially, close very often for the whole month. In September, literally from the last day of August actually you'll find the number of yachts competing for marina spaces and the numbers of boats in anchorages diminishes as if a switch has been flicked.

Many marinas have extended high season into September all the same and started it in July or even June in some cases, come October prices are generally more reasonable as marinas start to compete to try and persuade people to overwinter there.

There are many good marinas and a handful of bad. The best marina I experienced for friendly service was at Licata in Sicily. They didn't have much space on land, but I was able to get antifouling renewed at a nearby boatyard and the marina staff organised it for me. There are a number of marinas around Levkas and at the Gulf of Ambraccio for example, I in common with many liveaboards had my boat out of the water at Cleopatra marina to do some work on her and I had some good work done and sails made in Turkey.

The Fiumicino Canal near Rome has boatyards along both banks. I overwintered there one year, cheaply, and took the bus into Rome many times to explore the city and its museums and archaeology out of season. It was wonderful. The alternative is the marina at Ostia which is a pretty nice marina, just more expensive than the boatyards. That said the secret of the boatyards on the Fumicino Canal is out now, you'll need to book well ahead if you can and the prices won't be quite as cheap now. If you can get there ahead of your arrival by boat, on public transport from wherever else you may have stopped in Italy, to walk around and talk to people personally it'll probably help, as would a smattering of Italian.

I can't give you a list here, but look for places where you can get work done over winter, because if it's non emergency work that's the best time to do it. Talk to other sailors and consider returning to a place you know and trust if it's not too far. In most of Europe there's probably a marina or harbour of some sort every forty odd miles, so you do have choices and in low season they do have to compete for your business.

The key time is when you first buy your boat, it might be in a location that's suitable for you already. Had my offer been accepted right away on the Nicholson 38 at Eastbourne I'd have kept it there initially and had the work I needed, and also the work I wanted doing, done there. I ended up buying my boat in Waterford, in the Republic Of Ireland. Not handy when everything I wanted to put on board was in Kent in SE England.

As I mentioned before I chose Gravesend sailing Club and the canal basin as my starting point as it was primarily inexpensive and there were plenty of helpful and experienced club members. I did do some work on the boat there, but later had her lifted out at South Dock Marina in London for the bigger jobs, not as cheap, but better facilities.

If you're buying a boat with some months left on the marina fees it would be pointless to waste that. Living in just about any marina you'll meet people and hear where the good tradespeople can be found whatever speciality you need at the time, be it mechanical, electrical, carpentry, sailmaking etc.

I had my first set of new sails made by Gowen Ocean in Essex, that wasn't terribly close, but I still had a car in those days and I was happy with both the price and the workmanship. The chap I dealt with has retired now but I was impressed by his honesty, attitude and experience. If you feel comfortable dealing with someone it's a good start.

I've seen boats advertised as being ashore in a boatyard, so you might be buying a boat that's already in a boatyard on land, presumably if the vendor has had work done there, then he's established a rapport and degree of trust, but no harm in discussing it, with regard to any work you will want undertaken. Such places tend to be cheaper than marinas and the owner may or may not allow you to live on board while the boat is there. Some will see it as a form of security to have someone there, others will see it as unnecessary hassle to give you a key and access to the loos. Likewise they may, or may not, allow you to do the jobs you can do yourself on your own boat. It might work out, you might have to move on though.

When you check out a marina, especially that first one, make sure you can work on the boat yourself and that they don't dictate suppliers who they will, or wont allow through the gates.

Sometimes boats are advertised as being on a mooring. That can be cheap and if it doesn't dry out, and if there's somewhere safe to leave a dinghy ashore it could even be quite convenient as a spot to live, but little else.

If you're having a survey the boat will need to be moved to the nearest marina or harbour with lift out facilities and the lift out and survey will need to be booked to coincide obviously. You know there will be something you'll want to do after the survey if the sale completes. Even in the unlikely event the surveyor gives a one hundred percent clean bill of health, and I can't imagine that happens very often, you might want to renew anodes, apply fresh antifouling paint to the hull, or if planning to live aboard, as you apparently are, you might want to strip traditional anti fouling and replace it with something longer lasting such as Coppercoat. You might have made a shopping list having gone through the checklist, perhaps you want to install radar or AIS. There will be something even if it's just décor!

At the very least you'll want to move possessions and purchases on board and that's a hassle commuting in a small tender. Moorings are great and often cheap, but they can leave you a bit isolated at a time when you really want to be meeting and talking to other sailors and making new friends. In tidal areas moorings can dry out, leaving the boat nesting in mud you cannot wade through to reach her, so you're either trapped on board for some hours or can't go home, whatever the weather.

Make sure you choose a good marina with facilities, one which other sailors live at, or at least frequent. Look at several and if your first choice home is a long way from where the boat is currently, then get the vendor, or an experienced friend to make the trip with you. Your first journey in a strange boat should never be solo, even if you happen to be quite experienced. If you don't know anyone start asking around in the bar at the place you're leaving, and or the place you're going to. Sailors like to sail and they like to experience different types of boat, someone will be happy to make the trip.

Before you take that first long, solo voyage try to do a few legs with someone else aboard, just a second pair of hands makes a big difference when you start entering strange marinas, picking up a mooring, anchoring. I'm pretty experienced at doing all these things solo now, but time was it was a challenge and it will be for you if you're new to it. You need to be able to do these things in cross wind and currents and all sorts of varying conditions too. Don't be worried about that you'll learn, but don't rush to do it alone before you're ready.

In the modern day and age you'll be able to search for marinas online and you'll be able to get prices from the website too. It's likely that terms and conditions will be on the website and offers and deals, such as arrangements at other marinas within a group. If they have maintenance and repair facilities they'll be boasted about on the website. They may have tennis courts and a swimming pool even. Which if you need to meet people and make friends is no bad thing. Most have a bar and many a restaurant or cafe. They may advertise their in house brokerage and they may have a shop for everything from shackles to dinghies.

They may talk about CCTV and security guards, but I know one marina that made false claims in that regard and I was advised by a solicitor that if it's not written into the contract it's hard to pursue misleading advertising and actually get anywhere. Visit, see if the claims on the website match the reality. I'm still talking about your first marina here. I went into Gallions on my return to the UK in my boat I couldn't easily go ahead and check. (I realise I suggested that in the case of Fumicino, but it's really not practical as a regular way of life) You can, and really should check out your very first marina, before you commit.

Once you leave that first safe haven, the adventure really begins and could lead anywhere, so enjoy your time getting to know your boat and enjoy marina life, there will be times when perforce you're more of a recluse! By which I mean anchorages. I've written an entire book about anchoring and the implications of living at anchor. I once entered an anchorage on the southern coast of Sardinia and couldn't move or go ashore for several days such were the conditions, there is a video on my YouTube channel. Sailorsnook.

Start your boating life in a marina, but beautiful anchorages like this one below an ancient Greek temple await you.

On another occasion in The Mar Menor the conditions at anchor became so rough that I barely slept, set an audible alarm on the gps in case the boat took off while I was dozing and had to replace the anchor snubber, a bit of rope to absorb shocks better than the chain, about three or four times, again over about three days. Luckily that's two very memorable occasions in ten years. A well sheltered anchorage can be heavenly and if there are shops in dinghy commuting distance you may settle in for a while. In Mahon as mentioned before it's quite a long commute, but it's a jolly interesting place even before you find the Gin distillery.

Which almost wraps things up. I hope the complexities haven't scared you off. With research and proper planning and taking one day at a time you really can make this lifestyle work for you.

CHAPTER 15
THE LIVEABOARD LIFESTYLE – CONCLUSIONS

Living on board and travelling for most of the ten years that I owned my boat I met hundreds of people doing a similar thing. Many were retired, but I also met people of a similar age to me, I was forty seven when I started and I met people younger, as well as older, albeit younger people in somewhat smaller numbers, but it wasn't unheard of to meet couples with young children they were home schooling as the journeyed around the world.

I think that's a great education with the proviso that the kids get to have some time socialising with kids their own age. I did meet one young chap who appeared pretty depressed to me, having the constant company of adults, no sibling, no friends. Most of the people I met were very happy. Most were in couples. I did have a number of friends who came and visited and I'd like to thank David, Ken, Clive, Fiona, Gill, Gabriel, Martin, Freddy, Catherine and Dave, Steve, Daisy, Slaveia and Sara. Tragically for me two of my companions are no longer here, not as a result of sailing I hasten to add, but a reminder to live every day to the full.

There are many others I met and made friends with who were of course sailing their own boats. You can't keep in touch with everyone you meet, there will be hundreds, but a few have become good and lasting friends. What I learned in the long periods I was alone was that I can cope with my own company and enjoy myself, but that I'm actually a sociable person who likes human beings and that I'm happier not being alone as a general thing.

When you mix with others pursuing the same lifestyle it simply becomes normal and natural. Around the world thousands of people are doing it right now, if they can, you can, with the right preparation and a bit of money behind you and I hope this book has made you realise the possibilities not scared you away. For all that thousands of people do it, compared with the billions of people on the planet we're a very small minority. I use to fly home every Christmas, see family, do a bit of dancing and then fly back, it's only when you're back in 'normal' society that anyone thinks what you're doing is brave, out of the ordinary or bonkers, delete as appropriate.

If you still feel this lifestyle is for you, go get your RYA Day Skipper, start with an RYA Dinghy course if you don't know how a sailing boat functions. By the time you've got your Day Skipper practical you'll know how you feel about sailing. If you're still keen this book and the checklist which follows should help you to choose a boat that's ideal for you.

Photocopy or scan the checklist and enlarge it, print a few copies off. If scanning or copying isn't practical re-type it and print some, it's not so terribly long, but if you re-type it check and make sure you don't miss anything, the whole point of it is to make sure you ask everything you might possibly need to know and don't have to keep going back with more questions.

Fill them out, comparison is useful, does this boat really carry enough fresh water? This other one is the same size and it carries twice as much! It's not just as simple as ticking things off, of course it's highly likely to have water tanks, only very small boats carry plastic Jerry Cans for their water supply.

Some boats will have pretty much everything you need or want, right down to radar, AIS and solar panels, holding tanks, etc. Many others won't and if it's not there already you need to take account of the cost of making the boat a real genuine travelling liveaboard when you compare one with another. If you're pretty wealthy you might just buy the boat that appeals to you most and add a host
 of the things you need, but that's not most of us, the more it has to start with, providing it works, the better.

I was advised years ago by an old sailor at Key West when I was on holiday there just to jump in and learn as I went along, much as Shane Acton author of 'Shrimpy', who inspired me in my youth appears to have done. It's not quite in my nature, all my life I've taken risks, skydiving, single seater car racing, Supersport Motorcycle Racing, mountaineering and climbing, skiing and snowboarding, horse riding, starting a business, but I like to take calculated risks and I want to enjoy life a little longer.

The RYA may be shocked anyone would suggest this amount of sailing without a Yachtmaster qualification, I think highly of their courses and have recommended certain of them accordingly. I met few liveaboard boat gypsies with that level of qualification and I've not heard of any coming to grief which I probably would have given the bush telegraph. Of course it could happen, the sea is a very dangerous place and deserves your respect. Despite skydiving, and racing very fast motorcycles, I personally think long distance sailing is the most dangerous activity I've undertaken, but I know many sailors who think it's the safest thing I've done given the above list.

I have heard, in the media, of qualified Yachtmasters who have come to grief, the sea is no respecter of certificates. The level you go in at is up to you this is a discussion and I'm making suggestions based on my experience, I'm not dictating or even suggesting that my way is the only way. A full Yachtmaster course can be purchased for several thousand pounds, often with an ocean crossing built in, and if money is no object why not. They almost guarantee you'll pass, which might be a worry, but it's a business too many failures looks bad and is bad for custom.

I believe you can do it, but it's only an opinion, if after your Day Skipper Course You have nagging doubts take Coastal Skipper and if you still have doubts take the Yachtmaster by all means, if you have doubts after that or you've spent all your money best think again!

Don't forget to take your VHF radio licence, the radar course if you have radar and Sea Survival and First Aid. I took a comprehensive First Aid Kit and managed to get some broad spectrum antibiotics to carry as well, which I did need.

There comes a point where the talking has to stop and you have to get on with it. I'll suggest some useful and some plain old interesting reading now and hope you have a wonderful liveaboard life.

The pictures below show some of the rewards that await you.

The Corinth Canal

Minke Whale

Fishing boat at sunrise off Cartagena

Delos

Pilot whales

Eagle Owl taking a rest aboard off the coast of Portugal, can't guarantee you this particular experience, but if you spend enough time at sea you will experience avian visitors.

The Dutch canals

Octopus drying outside a restaurant in the Greek islands.

Stromboli at sunset.

Leaving your mark in The Azores.

Risso's Dolphin

Kayaking on the Guadiana River, if you take a kayak, or as I did an inflatable kayak.

A deserted anchorage on an uninhabited island! Yes really, uninhabited, a place where, if you're lucky and no one else sails in, you'll have it all to yourself. Paradise.

The Gulf of Corinth

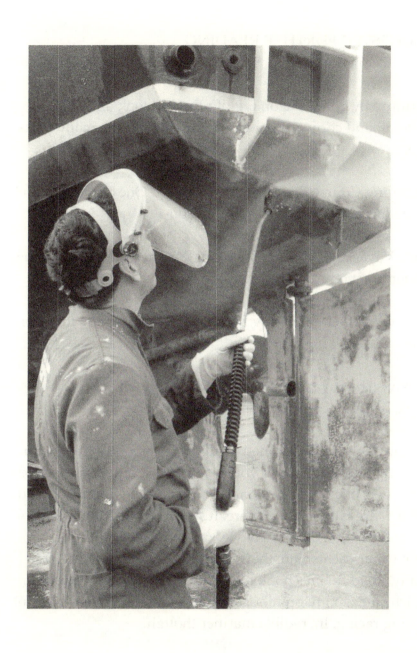

Oh, and some hard work!

SUGGESTED FURTHER READING

How To Anchor Safely – So You Sleep Well! By me. Of course!

Shrimpy By Shane Acton out of print but look online for a second hand copy or a download. It inspired me many years ago.

Changing Course By Debra Ann Cantrell One of the friends I made on my travels, living this lifestyle.

Lone Voyager By Maureen Jenkins Another friend and fellow writer I met on my travels.

Heavy Weather Sailing By K Adlard Coles the bible for storm survival.

Survive The Savage Sea By Dougal Robertson another old book, but an incredible story.

Sailing Alone Around The World By Captain Joshua Slocum the toughest old mariner you can imagine, but with a twinkle in his eye, one of my personal heroes and the first man to do what we're talking about here. It's a toss up between him and Robin Knox Johnson in my view as to who was the greatest blue water yachtsman, there are other candidates, but not many. Read Robin's book too by all means, it's far better than Chichister's in my opinion, but it's not on the list as we're not talking racing. Incredible mariner though.

If anyone wants to discuss my ideas for the ultimate World Explorer Yacht get in touch, I'm easy to find on Google, you'll need to be very wealthy to build it though.

Good Luck everyone get training and shopping!

BOAT FORM/CHECKLIST TO TAKE TO VIEWINGS SO YOU DON'T FORGET ANYTHING
(Take a camera too)

Name Of Boat
Location
Type Of Boat
Length Overall (LOA)   Beam   Draft
Asking Price
Owner's Contact Details
Broker Contact Details if applicable

Last Survey Date   Surveyor
Copy Provided

HULL

Date Last antifoul and anodes   Type of antifouling used

Number and location of anodes

Hull Material

Deck and superstructure material

Keel type   Rudder   Propeller
Type/Condition   Rope Cutter

ENGINE(S)/GEARBOX

Engine Type   Size   Age   Hours
Last service
Cooling type   Condition   Exhaust
type/condition
Spares carried on board

Visual check:
Cleanliness/leaks
Oil level
Oil change facilities/system
Cooling water level if applicable   anti freeze
Impeller if applicable
Condition hoses   condition belts
Stainless hose clips
Fuel filters   water separating
Fuel tank capacity
Consumption litres per hour   revs
speed   range
Instrumentation

Engine run yes/no   Oil pressure   Temperature
Ease of Starting
Smoke   water from exhaust
Starting Batteries type   number   clean/electrolyte level
isolator switch   battery rating

Wiring condition

Wing or auxiliary engine

Outboard bracket

Gearbox – check operation if engine run   forward   reverse   neutral

Hydraulic or mechanical

Condition of control cables

STEERING

Steering: Type Hydraulic   chain/cable   tiller

Check play   condition of chain cables   hydraulic levels   slippage if possible

BILGES

Condition of bilges   wet/dry   corrosion/paint

Pumps type number and operational (automatic switches?)
1
2
3
4

Bilge water alarms   Gas alarms CO_2 Alarm

EQUIPMENT/FEATURES/PLUMBING

Cooking system   Cooker type   condition   rings   grill   oven

If gas location of bottles (LPG/Calor/Propane), draining overboard

Condition and quality of hoses/pipes and age of rubber hoses
BS/ISO approved
Service record
Smoke alarm(s)
Fire Blanket

Fire extinguishers number   type   age
automatic system?
Type of extinguishant gas if in engine bay

Fridge type   operational

Type and condition of toilet(s)

Black water holding tank capacity   Pump out arrangements

Fresh water tank(s) number   capacity

Pumps electric AND manual/foot

Shore power cable and sockets   power points on board and type   Inverter
Wind generator   solar panels (rating)
Domestic batteries, number   type   condition   ampere hours

Shower Type   Pump works   Drain works
Hot water system(s)
Grey water tank

Navigational equipment
Auto pilot type   Operational
Radio type   Operational
Radar type   Operational
Depth sounder Type   Operational
AIS   Full   Read Only   Operational

Safety equipment:
Liferaft   Age   Last service date
Life jackets   Number   Type   Age/condition
Flares   Number   Type   Age
EPIRB
Search and rescue transponder
Radar reflector

Other Equipment And Fittings:

On deck
Locks and security
Handrail
Deck Fittings
Navigation lights working
Fog horn
Dan buoy
Man overboard recovery
Liferings/horseshoes/lights
Safety lines to clip on
Winches as applicable
Courtesy flags, Q Flag
Anchor Ball
Motoring Cone
Charts/Pilot Books

Mooring/Anchoring:

Bollards/cleats
Warps
Fenders
Passerelle
Anchor Type   Winch Type
Operational/condition
Chain   Size   Length   Mild or stainless steel
Spares (anchors, chain, warp)

Tender   Type   Age   Condition
Outboard motor(s)   Type   Age   Condition
Run (cooling water)
Last change of impeller

Miscellaneous:

General cosmetic appearance

Layout of accommodation sketch and description

Heating: Stove   Eberspacher/Webasto Type
Other
Fuel   Age
Condition   Service history

Available Storage

Berths number single   double   temporary

Inventory (what stays/what goes)

NOTES

ADDITIONAL FOR SAILING

Masts	Type		Condition	Age

Standing Rigging	Type		Condition	Age

Sails	No	Type	Age	Sail Area
Last valeted
1
2
3
4
5
6

Running Rigging			Age
Condition
Halyards
Sheets
Kicking strap(s)
Gybe control

Lazy Jacks or bag
Reefing system

Winches	Number	Type	Operational Condition
1			
2			
3			
4			
5			
6			

Cleats and jamming cleats
Spares

Documentation:

Registration Document

Receipt last time the boat changed hands/proof of ownership

VAT Paid (proof)   VAT Exempt (proof)   USA or other flag VAT to pay

Insurance   Value insured for   Cost of insurance   Co. insured with

Inland waterways permit if required

File of receipts for work done

Photographs from lift outs and of any work undertaken

Broker contract or private contract/RYA Sales Agreement

Deposit required

Sea or river trial as appropriate

Notes and observations from trial

DISCLAIMER

When you go to sea it is likely you will literally sink or swim based on the quality of your decision making at the time and when you make your preparations in advance. This book is based on a decade's worth of experience, however, whilst I believe wholeheartedly in the information I've provided for people to weigh up and consider I'm not endorsing any particular design, model or make of boat. I take no responsibility for the success or otherwise of adventures or purchases made by others, all choices are personal.

Copyright ©Malcolm Snook 2019

Made in the USA
Las Vegas, NV
25 September 2024

95766178R00173